# It's Time to Draw the Line!

## What Parents Must Do Now to Save Our Children and Restore Our National Treasure

**Richard L. Hudson**

Belief Investing Media

Belief Investing Media
A Division of Belief Incorporated
3225 South McLeod Drive, Suite 100
Las Vegas, NV 89121
USA

**It's Time to Draw the Line!**

*What Parents Must Do Now to Save Our
Children and Restore Our National Treasure*

Belief Investing, Belief Ability, BeliefBank, BeliefBanker,
Belief Bankruptcy, Belief-Based Guidance System,
Belief Portfolio, Belief Leadership, Managing Beliefs,
The Ultimate Legacy, The Most Important Investment
You'll Ever Make, Great Ultimate Legacy Paradox, The
Three Life Lines, and Speak Your Mind—Without
Losing It are trademarks of WordCache, LLC.

Belief Investing Media is a trademark
of Belief Incorporated.

Manufactured in the United States of America

*It's Time to Draw the Line!* is a component
of the Belief Investing™ Series.

ISBN-13: 978-0-9845504-0-1

SDG        BI-DRAW-B-10/10

# Contents

# Part Two
## Developing Your Belief Ability™

# Part Three
## Discovering Your Role

# Part Four
## Drawing The Three Life Lines™

# Introduction

In 2010, the United States is in a deficit crisis. Almost daily we see signs that the nation is moving closer to total bankruptcy and a devastating crash. Yet few seem willing to acknowledge the danger or do anything about it.

You may think I am talking about the national debt, the entitlement explosion, or the looming financial meltdown. Although the financial situation is of serious concern, it is *merely a symptom* of a much more important deficit—the erosion of our national morality. It's a case of what I call Belief Bankruptcy™.

**"What are the minimum moral requirements needed for the nation to hold together?"**

A few weeks ago, I asked this question of an editor from a prestigious national weekly newsmagazine. A perplexed look and a long silence followed. "I . . . I don't know," the editor finally said. "It's a good question."

It's a question that is hard to answer specifically. It seems that each new day, we see and hear more evidence that we need to *ask* the question. And for the sake of our nation and our children, we need to *answer* it.

In a recent Gallup Poll (May 3–6, 2010) 76% of respondents said that moral values in the United States are getting worse. This annual poll on moral values found "current ratings rank among the worst Gallup has measured over the past nine years."

Of course, you probably didn't need a Gallup Poll to tell you that. If you watch the news each day, you see it for yourself. And you see the effects on your kids.

### What are Tiger Woods, Bernie Madoff, John Edwards, Jesse James, and other public figures teaching our children?

Scoundrels, rip-off artists, and serial liars have been around for a long time. Why the concern now? We now have a 24-hour news cycle. It feeds on celebrity, scandal, personal misfortune, and controversy. The stories appear over and over again in more forms of media than ever before. Our children get a concentrated, toxic mix of evasion, lies, and broken promises—often from people who have been celebrated in the media. What is *that* teaching our kids?

How do we protect our kids from this toxic atmosphere?

### The *antidote* for public figures who lie and break their promises is parents who tell the truth and keep their promises.

The real solution for the morality deficit is parents who teach their children well—parents who teach their children the morals, values, and character that will rebuild our national morality.

If the nation is to be saved, today's parents need to do it. You need to do it by arming yourself with powerful beliefs and by living them. And you need to teach those beliefs to your children so they can live them now and in the future.

### You can do this!

You can make a difference in the life of your child. No matter how old he or she is, you can use your influence and see a change. Really, you can do this.

The purpose of this book is to encourage, equip, and empower parents to build the powerful beliefs behind strong morals, values, and character. It's written for parents and for those who support them—teachers, pastors, youth workers, friends, and especially, grandparents. Right now parents *need* our support—our encouragement and prayers.

You are unlikely to find typical parenting advice here. My expertise is in beliefs and in how they operate in our lives. The principles in this book can change your life now. And *your* changed life can change your child's. How do I know? I've spend 15 years as an executive coach teaching these principles to CEOs and Managing Directors in 14 countries on 4 continents. I've seen lives and whole companies changed by the power of these principles.

You may have heard or read something about beliefs, but it's likely you haven't been told the whole truth. In Chapter 4, we'll clear up three big misconceptions about beliefs, so you can start to access their power. The more you read the more you'll become fascinated and curious about the role of beliefs in your life.

Have you tried to make changes in your life, get rid of habits, start something new, only to find frustration and failure? In this book, you'll learn how ignoring your beliefs can block change and how you can set a new, more powerful course. That's in Chapter 6.

Do you think that being a parent is all about sacrificing for your child? You'll learn about what I call the GULP—the Great Ultimate Legacy Paradox™. This concept in Chapter 7 will challenge how you think about the role you play in your child's life.

Once you experience the power of beliefs in your own life, you'll be eager to teach your child how to use these same simple principles. How do you get his or her attention? See Chapter 8 to read about three things you need to increase your influence with your child.

**The beliefs we hold have *everything* to do with the development of morality, values, and character.**

Later on, in Chapters 10-12, you'll learn a simple yet profound process, The Three Life Lines™. Draw these lines to teach your child about morality, values, and character.

You and your child face a battle. Throughout the book you'll learn about your competition—about all those wanting to direct, distort, and even dominate your child's thinking. You'll read about two special weapons you, as a parent, have in the battle for your kid's beliefs, and how you can use them to your best advantage.

Just as this book was going to press, a new Internet assault on children came to light, but was largely ignored by the media. So I added the Postscript describing the danger and pointing you toward some defensive tools with which to arm your children to withstand the attacks on their beliefs.

Understand that we face nothing less than an all-out battle for the hearts and minds of our children and the survival of our nation. It's a battle we *can* win. It's a battle we *must* win.

**It's time to draw the line!**

# But Wait; There's More!

**This book is only part of what I've put together for you.** My hope is that you will be increasingly successful with your children, so I have some additional resources waiting for you. These are free to purchasers of *It's Time to Draw the Line!*

**Demo Video**   First, you can watch a demonstration video that will show how to use many of the concepts presented here. Long after you finish reading this book, the video can remind you of what you can say and do to teach your children about beliefs, morality, values, and character. Access the video at:

**http://www.ICanDrawTheLine.com/demo**

**Webinars**   Second, you can access webinars in which I present additional resources for parents. In these webinars, you'll get more ideas, cutting edge strategies, to help you build powerful beliefs to pass on to your children. To register for these free webinars, go to:

**http://www.ICanDrawTheLine.com/webinars**

I hope that you will use and enjoy these additional resources. I wish only the best for you and your family!

*RLHudson*

# A Note from the Author

"In the event of a loss of cabin pressure, oxygen masks will be deployed from the panel above you. Make sure you put your mask on first, and then assist any children who might be accompanying you."

How many times have you heard that?

This book is written based on a belief that comes from more than 20 years of studying beliefs: Just as you can't give away property you don't own, you can't give away beliefs you don't own.

With that in mind, I present ideas throughout this book on how to build your beliefs and pass them on to your children.

Understand that the proper sequence is to "put your mask on first" and then to "assist your children."

## Part One

# Defending the Boundaries

*If we are to go forward, we must go back*

*and rediscover those precious values—that*

*all reality hinges on moral foundations*

*and that all reality has spiritual control.*

—**Martin Luther King, Jr.**

# CHAPTER 1

# Who's Drawing the Lines, and Why Aren't They Listening to You?

## To Set a Boundary, Draw a Line

What if it were possible to build powerful, positive, life-changing beliefs to set boundaries for you and your children—and restore boundaries for the nation? That's what this book can do.

Why is setting those boundaries so important? Consider what's happening to children and parents in our country . . .

The headline said, "Mother furious after in-school clinic sets up teen's abortion."

As reported by KOMO News online service, the story explained how the school issued a pass to a 15-year-old, put her in a taxi, and sent her off to have an abortion during school hours without her mother knowing.

The school defended itself by saying that the girl's mother had signed a consent form for her daughter to go to the Ballard Teen Health Center, located inside the school, for medical care. But the mother had no idea that this signature would allow her child to be sent off-campus and to receive an abortion without her knowledge.

It turns out that parents' rights didn't matter. T.J. Cosgrove, of the King County Health Department responsible for the school-based health programs, says parents don't have a say: "At any age in the state of Washington, an individual can consent to a termination of pregnancy."

A commenter on a blog that was discussing this story pointed out that parents of a girl this age could be put in jail for neglect, yet they have no control over their child's decisions or over the school and the state's decisions, all of which superseded their parental rights.

What line protects parents' rights to raise their children?

It's time to draw the line!

In the *New York Times*, Op-Ed Columnist Maureen Dowd tells of a fantasy sex league started by ninth grade boys at the all-boys private Landon Upper School in the wealthy Washington suburb of Bethesda, MD. Dowd says the boys planned a fantasy football-like draft in which female students at other local schools were chosen for each "team" and "points" were to be scored on the basis of sexual encounters with these girls.

Dowd went on to quote Jean Erstling, the director of communications at Landon: "Landon has an extensive ethics and character development education program which includes as its key tenets respect and honesty. Civility toward women is definitely part of that education program."

Apparently it's not working. How do parents and schools really teach ethics and character?

It's time to draw the line!

The failure of boundaries is not just affecting our children. We can see it more each day in other parts of our lives.

The San Joaquin Valley in California has been called America's Garden of Eden. Almost 13% of the produce grown in the United States comes from this area. Or, it did.

Over the last few years, farmers in the San Joaquin Valley have found their water allotments drying up. Now, fields are left unplanted. Orchards are dry, and trees are withering. Crop yields have plummeted, and shipments of produce out of the area have dwindled. Unemployment in much of the valley has risen to 40%, one of the highest rates in the country. Families line up at local food banks to collect food—imported from China.

Why is this happening? Is the San Joaquin Valley experiencing a massive drought? Is global warming changing the weather patterns? Is the water gone?

No. There's enough water for the crops, but the federal government has diverted it to save an endangered species of fish: the Delta Smelt. Fish get the water that once supported thousands of farmers. Our government has created a modern-day dustbowl by putting the well-being of a bait fish before humans'.

This is just one example of government bureaucrats moving the boundaries despite the human cost.

It's time to draw the line!

You've probably heard and read about stories like these, and maybe some that are even more outrageous. But they have a different impact when you experience, as I did, the erosion of boundaries wrapped in an appealing offer.

A few weeks ago, I listened to a teleseminar about reducing credit-card debt. It seems that a law firm has found a way to take more than 60% of one's credit-card debt and make it go away. After I heard a few details, I hung up. The next day, someone else from the organization called and asked if I wanted to get in on the program. I asked a question neither had addressed: "The debt doesn't just go away—who takes the hit?"

"Oh, it's the credit card company that takes the hit," the caller said.

"Why would they be willing to do that?" I asked.

The answer: "Because they'd rather get some of their money and get the debt off the books." The caller then asked, "Are you ready to sign up?"

I said, "Well, I know you may not understand this, but any credit-card bills I have are from real expenditures I made. That is *my* debt, and I am responsible for it. I think it is reprehensible for a person to make someone else take the hit for my debt just because you found a loophole. It may be possible, it may be legal, but it is morally wrong."

The caller didn't seem to understand, so I went on. "So, if I buy this service and pay you with my credit card, and then the debt gets dismissed, you don't mind not getting your money, right?"

He said, "That's the beauty of this loophole. My company gets our money, and the credit card company takes the hit."

When I asked him if he thought that was right, the caller started back into his pitch, telling me I must not really understand the program. But I did understand— I understood it all too well.

What the caller couldn't understand is that I know how to draw lines, and that was a line I refused to cross.

Although I haven't always been consistent at recognizing and drawing them, I understand today, more than ever, the importance of drawing bright, clear lines.

As I said, I have a vision of what this book can do. You can restore powerful, positive, life-changing beliefs that will set boundaries for you and your children— and restore boundaries for the nation. Which leads me to one of the primary beliefs behind this book:

*Decide, draw, and defend your own boundaries, or someone else will do it for you.*

## The History of Line Changing

For years, some people around us—in government, the media, universities, and even some religious organizations—have had a lot to say about lines. At times they've said these things quietly, behind the scenes, but consistently they whisper about changing or erasing the lines.

One of my first encounters with line-changers was with Abbie Hoffman's book *Steal This Book*. I was young and curious about what he had to say, so I bought a copy. (Yes, I *bought* it, despite the title encouraging shoppers to step across a line and rip it off.) The book openly encouraged young people to do away with most of the lines in their lives, especially those drawn or defended by anyone older than 30.

In that book I first recognized evidence of a movement dedicated to change—changing the lines. Since then I have seen people:

Blurring the line
Shading the line
Claiming there is no line
Making fun of the lines
Covering the line
Rubbing out the line
Ignoring the line
Reasoning away the line
Walking around the line
Pretending there is no line

My wife did a search in stock-photo galleries for images portraying people who recognized and respected boundaries. She found that most of the photos showed people stepping across lines and triumphantly breaking through boundaries.

Please understand: I recognize that some boundaries need to be broken through.

Much of my work in the last two decades has been helping people break through self-imposed limiting beliefs. Some of my work has been about teaching people how to recognize limits imposed by other people and how to break through them. Many boundaries on what we can do or say *need* to be broken. We need to push the boundaries of the human spirit and champion what we can accomplish as individuals.

I also understand that we should change boundaries when lines are drawn in the wrong places. In the past, lines were drawn about what race or gender one needed to be to vote. Lines were drawn about what neighborhoods one could live in, or where one could sit in a bus or at a lunch counter. Those lines largely have been erased, and new lines have been drawn to include differences in race and gender. The new lines were declarations that freedom and opportunity needed to be inclusive.

But some boundaries *are* drawn in the right places, even if they are sometimes inconvenient and uncomfortable. For example, driving 20 miles per hour in a school zone is seldom convenient, but there is a good reason for that boundary.

At first, the people I noticed who advocated getting rid of the lines were isolated and on the fringe. More and more, those voices have become organized. Many have been accepted as mainstream. The rebellion and lawlessness of the 60s and 70s have become an everyday part of today's culture.

What we see today is an attempt to erase or ignore *more* lines. One group of global anarchists would like nothing better than to wipe out all lines. They show up at meetings of the World Bank and other high-profile global events to demonstrate. Some even showed up in February of 2010 in Vancouver, British Columbia, for the Winter Olympics. They paraded through streets, breaking windows and throwing bricks. They had no discernible demands other than to abolish all law and authority. They seem to think the ensuing chaos will give rise to some better form of government, so they want to abolish all control.

Today many seem willing to draw lines to limit your freedom and mine, while ignoring or erasing lines that limit their power. Some say that we really need experts to make decisions to guide the nation, that ordinary citizens can't make policy decisions. All the while, out of sight, they lift, shift, or erase the lines that have protected our freedoms. That's why they aren't listening. And this is supposed to be for our own good.

I'm not a political scholar, so I'll say little more about these movements other than to repeat:

*Decide, draw and defend your own boundaries, or someone else will do it for you.*

Where did this line-changing start? Actually, it was not very long after the first lines were drawn.

The campaign against boundaries and rules has been around for a long time. The Judeo-Christian tradition holds that sin entered the world because of the violation of a clear boundary. In Genesis, God tells Adam that he and Eve are free to eat the fruit of any tree in the Garden of Eden but one—the Tree of the Knowledge of Good and Evil. God set a boundary. He drew a line. God then defended that boundary by saying that anyone who ate from that tree would surely die.

The Tempter went after Adam and Eve and tried to subvert each of these points.

First, the Tempter asked, did God really say *that*? So the first tactic was to question the boundary.

Second, the Tempter said, "You won't really *die.*" This tactic was designed to mitigate results of crossing the boundary. The Tempter gives no evidence and no reasons, but the statement alone was enough to cast doubt on the reality of the consequences.

Third, the Tempter said, "Don't you understand? God just wants to keep you stupid. He knows that if you eat that fruit you'll be as smart as He is." Here the Tempter reinterprets the meaning of the boundary by questioning the motive of the line-drawer, implying that God is not all He's cracked up to be, and that, in fact, the boundary is to keep Adam and Eve from attaining their full potential. (I've paraphrased the Tempter's words from Genesis 2:16–17.)

Whether you believe the account of what happened in the Garden of Eden or not, you will find that the tactics outlined above are the same ones that line-changers have used throughout history:

- Question the boundary.
- Question the consequences of breaking the boundary.
- Question the integrity and motives of the boundary maker.

I'm not saying that all line-changers are evil, are acting out of some nefarious motivation, or are being subversive. Many act out of good motives but are unaware of the unintended consequences of their actions. And, in truth, some lines *do* need to be changed, such as the old racial discrimination laws that have been erased.

## Boundaries under Siege

All around us, our boundaries are being challenged.

Boundaries are being challenged in our schools: What goes in textbooks and what gets left out? Should the Federal government have control over local education? Are schools asserting rights that should be left to parents?

Boundaries are being challenged in our churches. Churches are divided over who can serve in leadership roles: What about women? Non-celibate homosexuals? Some deny the major doctrines the Christian church has held throughout history.

Boundaries are being challenged in our businesses. Government takes over banks, school loan funding, health care, and a big chunk of the automobile business. Government tries to take over control of the Internet, but is stopped, at least temporarily, by the courts. Who should manage the Internet, if anyone?

Boundaries are being challenged in our personal lives. Personal property rights are under attack. Government exerts its muscle, which leads to families getting thrown out of their homes by Eminent Domain—a law that says land could only be taken for government use, but that is used now to take land so the government can sell it to developers. Privacy is under attack as surveillance cameras in some cities watch your every move. Speed and stoplight cameras attempt to enforce laws. What about the right of individuals to face an accuser? Can you own a firearm? Can you speak freely?

The issues here are not simply that the boundaries are being challenged. The questions asked are valid because:

- You *need* to consider the reasons for the boundary.
- You *need* to consider the consequences of breaking the boundary.
- And most of all, you *need* to consider the integrity and motives of the boundary maker.

You *need* to be asking those questions of yourself and of others. Why? It's because *you* will be asked those questions, and *your* boundaries will be challenged. You need to know the answers for yourself. Your children will be asked those questions, and they need answers with which to defend themselves. These questions will be asked about our nation, and we need to be able to answer them for all of us.

In other words, *it's time to draw the line!*

Two things make that clear:

First, the questioning of our lines and boundaries, our beliefs and values, our history and our laws, is coming ever more quickly. The pace and influence of line-changers is increasing, and we are seeing the effects of line changes all around us.

Second, it is becoming more and more difficult for parents to teach the answers to those questions. Many who had been teaching the answers—in our schools, churches and synagogues, the government and media—now are actively on the side of challenging the answers.

If you doubt this, recall the words of Rep. Alcee Hastings, a member of the House of Representatives Rules Committee, commenting on the Obamacare legislation: "I wish I had been there when Thomas Edison made the remark that I think applies here: 'There ain't no rules around here, we're trying to accomplish something.' And therefore, when the deal goes down, all this talk about rules, we make them up as we go along." Maybe he didn't take seriously his oath to uphold and defend the Constitution of the United States of America.

Rep. Hastings, it should be noted, was formerly a federal judge who was impeached, tried, and removed from the bench by the U.S. Senate. Only six judges in American history have ever been removed this way. In spite of that dishonor, Hastings was elected to the House of Representatives and rose to membership in the House Rules Committee.

Your children will make their own decisions about what to believe. Who will provide them with the information to make those decisions?

Parents, who bear the ultimate responsibility for teaching their children, are finding it more difficult than ever to find time to do so.

You may have good answers for the questions raised in this chapter, but with the competition for the hearts and minds of your children and the limited time you have, it may not be that easy to pass along the beliefs, values, and character traits so necessary for them to defend their boundaries.

The result is that today we find fewer and fewer people willing or able to do the very thing that needs to be done—draw a line.

What we are experiencing as a result of the failure to draw and reinforce boundaries is the growth of what I call Belief Bankruptcy™.

## Beliefs to Consider

At the end of each chapter, I highlight some of the beliefs discussed in it. Take a few moments to read them and consider what they mean for you.

- Just as you can't give away property you don't own, you can't give away beliefs you don't own.
- You can build your beliefs and pass them on to your children.
- To set a boundary, draw a line.
- Decide, draw, and defend your own boundaries, or someone else will do it for you.
- Some people around us—in government, the media, universities, and even some religious organizations—have been working to change the lines.
- We need to push the boundaries of the human spirit and what we can accomplish as individuals.
- Boundaries need to change when lines are drawn in the wrong places.

- The campaign against boundaries and rules has been around for a long time.
- Line-changers have used these tactics throughout history:
  — Question the boundary.
  — Question the consequences of breaking the boundary.
  — Question the integrity and motives of the boundary maker.
- You will be asked these questions, and your boundaries will be challenged, so:
  — You *need* to consider the intent of the boundary.
  — You *need* to consider the consequences of breaking the boundary.
  — And most of all, you *need* to consider the integrity and motives of the boundary maker.
- The pace and influence of the line-changers is increasing, and we are seeing the effects of line changes all around us.
- Many who have been charged with teaching the answers to these questions—in schools, our churches and synagogues, the government, and the media—are actively on the side of challenging the answers.
- Your children will make their own decisions about what to believe.

# CHAPTER 2

# Our Nation's Looming Deficit Disaster—Belief Bankruptcy™

A few years ago, I coined the term Belief Bankruptcy™. The term didn't feel good, but it was the best way to describe the phenomenon.

The term came to mind after an event that was reported internationally. It was a so-called powder-puff football game between high school senior and junior girls from Glenbrook North High School. But the game was just the backdrop for brutal hazing, with the senior girls dumping paint, pig intestines, and human feces over the heads of the junior girls, while beating them up. The violence sent several girls to the hospital—one with a broken ankle, another with a broken rib, and several suffering severe concussions. A dozen or so others were badly beaten but were treated and released.

All this occurred in an upscale suburb where 98% of the students go on to college. Reportedly, three dozen participants were suspended from school and criminally cited for misdemeanor battery. Two mothers of the girls were cited for providing alcohol to minors. (Parents of several of the girls later sent them on a cruise to escape media attention.)

People across the country raised many questions: How could kids from great schools, good neighborhoods, and affluent families act this way? How could they be brutal to fellow students? How could they show so little regard for others?

In short, *how could this happen?*

I asked a different question: "What beliefs must be in place for this kind of behavior to be seen as okay?"

This incident prompted me to think about the *beliefs* held by the girls involved. Seeing the apparent absence of restraining beliefs, I coined the term "Belief Bankruptcy™."

"Belief Bankruptcy™? Isn't that a little strong?" you may ask.

Call it "Belief Bankruptcy™" or a "values void"; those kids brutalized others and did it for fun. Their actions showed a lack of restraining beliefs and values.

Others said, "These kids must have known, at some level, that what they were doing was wrong."

Yes, I think they did know the behavior was wrong—but *they did it anyway!* At some level, they *decided* it was okay to participate in a brutal hazing even if it was wrong.

So what belief made *that* possible? Where did they learn that? These girls were willing to cross or ignore some serious lines.

That realization scared me, and I wouldn't be surprised if it scared you, too.

When I have told others about the Glenbrook hazing story, some have asked who is to blame. They seem concerned that maybe I'll point to the parents. Yes, the parents get some of the blame.

A friend of mine was in a leadership position at that school. Year after year my friend heard parents deflecting responsibility away from their kids—even to the point of insulating them from the natural consequences of their actions. For example, when a boy was caught with a cheat sheet in hand during a test, his parents said the paper wasn't his. Not only did they deny their son had done anything wrong, they actually claimed he was being a good citizen by picking up a paper that someone else had thrown on the floor!

Yes, the parents get some of the blame in these cases. But I don't think that the hazing was entirely the parents' fault. I've already described some of the other willing accomplices—all the people who encouraged line-changing, people who helped these girls ignore or blur the line.

Since then, I have realized that Belief Bankruptcy™ is spreading because of the inability or unwillingness of people to draw lines. It's not a bankruptcy *of* beliefs—everyone has beliefs. Instead it is a bankruptcy *because of* beliefs—beliefs that allow one to ignore or cross important lines.

Fortunately, you can draw the line and stop Belief Bankruptcy™. It starts with you. You can build powerful beliefs in your life, you can influence your children, and you can restore the national morality.

You can do this. I'll show you how.

## Beliefs to Consider

- You can discover a lot by asking, "What beliefs must be in place for this kind of behavior to be okay?"
- Belief Bankruptcy™ is spreading because of the inability or unwillingness of people to draw lines.
- Belief Bankruptcy™ is a bankruptcy *because of* beliefs—beliefs that allow one to ignore or cross important lines.

# CHAPTER 3

# The Lines that Transformed
# the World

Fortunately, the United States has a history of people willing to draw lines—and that was the genius of our Founding Fathers: they knew how to draw lines. They'd personally seen how the failure to draw lines during King George's rule led to the loss of their freedom.

The Founders knew from history of decisive moments when bright, clear lines had been drawn: God giving the Ten Commandments, Jesus giving the Great Commandment, and the signing of the Magna Carta in 1215.

Then on July 4, 1776, the Founders drew another bright, clear line with the Declaration of Independence.

It marked the beginning of the golden age of drawing lines, which culminated with the writing of the U.S. Constitution and the Bill of Rights.

Our nation was defined by the Founding Fathers who knew how to decide, draw, and defend lines.

They recognized lines between right and wrong.

They recognized lines between states.

They drew lines between the branches of government.

They drew lines between personal and government responsibility.

They recognized lines between God-given rights and government-granted privileges.

They drew lines between civilian and military authority.

They recognized lines between personal and government property.

They drew lines to protect freedom of speech.

By recognizing and formalizing the existing lines and by drawing new lines, the Founding Fathers set boundaries around our rights and freedoms.

In my travels around the world, I've talked with many people who miss the real importance of those lines. The line in the Declaration saying, "they are endowed by their Creator with certain unalienable rights, that among these are Life, Liberty, and the pursuit of Happiness," doesn't seem to register with everyone. Many people don't seem to understand that our rights come from *God*, not from the government.

Why *would* they understand? The only rights they have experienced have been granted by their governments.

Few Americans seem to grasp the importance of Thomas Jefferson's words:

*Government big enough to supply everything you need is big enough to take everything you have. The course of history shows us that as a government grows, liberty decreases.*

Much of the turmoil in our country today is because we have lost sight of the lines. There are those who have told us over and over that there are no lines (except where they draw them). They say that the lines drawn by the Founders either do not mean what we think they mean or that they're not relevant for today. They say there is "no controlling legal authority" and then use the court system to force change not possible by the rightful legislative process.

## Public and Private Virtue

One of the Founding Fathers who was among the best at understanding and drawing lines was John Adams. He wrote:

> *The foundation of national morality must be laid in private families . . . Public virtue cannot exist in a nation without private, and public virtue is the only foundation of republics.*

I believe this public and private virtue is our *true* national treasure. This treasure, as Adams says, is laid in private families.

These beliefs and values that constitute our national treasure provide a basis for trust—in each other and in our government. What happens to this trust if these beliefs and values are not present? The latest Pew Research Center poll (April 19, 2010) shows nearly 8 in 10 Americans don't trust the federal government.

Just 22% say they can trust Washington. What does that say about our national treasure? Where is the basis for trust—the consent of the governed?

In 1772, Adams wrote in his diary:

> *The Preservation of Liberty depends on the intellectual and moral Character of the People. As long as Knowledge and Virtue are diffused generally among the Body of a Nation, it is impossible they should be enslaved. This can be brought to pass only by debasing their Understandings, or by corrupting their Hearts.*

Here is a question to think about: Is the Belief Bankruptcy™ we see today the result of debased understandings, or the result of hearts that are corrupted? I think that debased understanding *leads* to the corrupting of hearts. What do you think?

So what has happened to public and private virtue, the foundation of our national morality? Unfortunately, virtue is rarely taught in our homes. Why? I believe there are several reasons.

First, I believe parents tell themselves that their children learn public virtues at school. Parents look to teachers to teach morality, values, and character. But a look at textbooks shows that little is actually being done to teach national morality.

A hundred years ago—even forty years ago—schools tried to teach beliefs and values in civics and citizenship classes. But at some point, it seems teaching other topics became more important. There's a lot of environmental education, and sex education, and diversity education, but how much do students learn about the "Knowledge and Virtue" of which John Adams spoke?

Second, all too often, parents who do try to teach good beliefs and values to their children face massive competition. A steady stream of words, images, and examples from the media and culture teaches children that they can choose any lines they want—or none at all. The number and volume of voices competing with parents is enormous: TV, movies, books, magazines, music, video games, Internet sites, Twitter, Facebook, MySpace. They're all after your children's hearts and minds.

Many of the competing voices aren't amateurs sending some vague message. They are seasoned professionals—advertisers, script writers, video-game developers, producers, publishers, editors, and even school administrators and teachers. They have "gone to school" on how to impact, influence, and instill beliefs and values in your children.

The third big reason that virtue isn't being taught is that many parents simply don't know what to say and do. If you are in that boat—you want to make sure your kids learn public and private virtue but don't know what to do or say—know that your situation is probably not your fault. You may not be entirely clear about your own beliefs and values, because *you* probably weren't taught them either.

About all that today's parents have had to go on is the example set by their parents. Even if your parents were good at teaching their beliefs and values to you, the climate of communication has changed. What your parents did to teach you won't cut it today. As a parent, you must be assertive if you hope to retain or reclaim your influence with your children.

One way to develop that influence is by winning the right to be heard. We'll cover that in another chapter. For additional thoughts about influence, you can download my free Special Report, *7 Ways to be a Hero in Your Home,* at http://www.HeroInYourHome.com.

Interestingly, John Adams predicted times very much like the ones in which we find ourselves now. In a letter to his wife, Abigail, written in 1776, Adams acknowledged that there might be troubles ahead for the emerging nation. He wrote:

> *America shall suffer Calamities still more wasting and Distresses yet more dreadfull . . . If this is to be the Case, it will have this good Effect, at least: it will inspire us with many Virtues, which We have not, and correct many Errors, Follies, and Vices, which threaten to disturb, dishonor, and destroy Us.*

In other words, John Adams thought that calamities and distresses would inspire us to virtues and cause us to correct our errors, follies, and vices.

Whether he was right about this remains to be seen. That depends on the ability of parents to prepare themselves and their children for the challenges of the next few decades.

I recognize the challenges parents face today. You shouldn't have to face the challenge of teaching your children alone, but teaching them is not the *responsibility* of others. You should have the *support* of your friends. You should have the *support* of your church. You should have the *support* of your school—the teachers, the administration, and the PTO or PTA. You should have support, but for many of you this book may be all you have to start with.

The issue is important enough to start alone if you have to. However, once you begin, you'll find others who see the same things and feel the same way you do.

How do you draw the right kinds of lines for yourself and teach your children to do the same? The next few chapters talk about beliefs—what they are, how they are developed, and how to pass them on. You'll find simple steps to put into practice in the process of just loving and caring for your children.

## Beliefs to Consider

- The genius of our Founding Fathers was that they knew how to draw lines.
- Our rights come from God and not from government.
- The Founders drew a bright, clear line with the Declaration of Independence.
- The Declaration marked the beginning of the golden age of drawing lines—followed by the U.S. Constitution, including the Bill of Rights.

- The Founding Fathers set boundaries around our rights and freedoms.
- A government that grants rights can just as easily take them away.
- Public and private virtue is our true national treasure.
- Parents tell themselves that public virtue is taught in school.
- Parents who do try to teach good beliefs and values to their children face massive competition.
- Many parents don't know what to do or say to teach their children public and private virtue.

Part Two

---

# Developing Your Belief Ability™

*If you believe you can, you probably*

*can. If you believe you won't, you most*

*assuredly won't. Belief is the ignition*

*switch that gets you off the launching pad.*

—**Denis Waitley**

# Belief Ability™

In Part Two, you'll find three sets of questions to help you develop Belief Ability™—your ability to use beliefs. I'll provide some of the answers, and some you'll answer for yourself.

First . . . What are beliefs? How are beliefs defined? How do beliefs form? How do beliefs operate in our lives?

Second . . . How do beliefs work in your life? How do beliefs shape what you say and do? How do beliefs affect your children?

Third . . . How do you choose and change beliefs? How do you invest in beliefs that work for you rather than against you? How do you use beliefs to bring you the results that you want, now and in the future? How do you pass on beliefs to your children?

On to Part Two to understand what beliefs are, how they operate, and how you can put them into action.

# Chapter 4

# Unlocking the Power Behind the Secret

For more than 20 years, I have studied beliefs and how they impact our lives.

Discussing beliefs with people can be a bit strange. At first, they are unsure of what I mean by beliefs. They ask, "What's *your* definition of beliefs?" and, "Is this going to be a discussion of religion?" Those questions are understandable.

As conversations progress, people begin to get excited about how understanding beliefs gives them power.

A friend of mine is a musician and teacher. He came to me one day, saying that what he'd learned from me about beliefs had totally changed the way he works with his students. "It's amazing," he said. "Beliefs, behavior, results. It works every time!" (In Chapter 6, you'll learn why he was so excited.)

As you learn more about beliefs and how they operate in your life, you'll be tempted to ask, "Why didn't someone tell me about this sooner? Why has this been such a secret?"

This book lets you in on the secret.

Folks typically have three misconceptions about beliefs:

First, that beliefs are some mysterious theological or philosophical stuff that should be left to scholars and theologians.

Second, that messing around with beliefs is somehow off-limits, like attempting to change the operating system on your computer. They think that sure, you might get in there, but if you touch the wrong thing, you could crash the whole program.

Third, that even if you could get in there to examine your beliefs, that they're too hard to change, so why bother?

Let's take those misconceptions one at a time.

Misconception 1: *Beliefs are mysterious theological or philosophical stuff that should be left to scholars and theologians.*

## Understanding Managing Beliefs™

True, some beliefs are theological and philosophical, but most are extremely down-to-earth. Beliefs are simply the mental programs, the "rules of thumb" we use to run our everyday lives. They are what I call Managing Beliefs™.

They allow you to do something, almost on autopilot, while paying attention to something else. Beliefs are the underlying human programming, the rules that keep us safe, operating correctly, and on course for what we want in our lives, even when we can't afford to be thinking about it.

For example, if you grew up in the Americas, you have probably developed the Managing Belief™ that the correct way to drive is on the right side of the road. This is deeply ingrained in your being, even if you don't drive a car. You don't even think about it—you probably haven't thought about it in months, or maybe even years. But virtually every day, without fail, you act on this belief.

This belief affects your behavior and helps keep you safe when you drive. It even affects you when you walk down a hallway or down a crowded sidewalk. When someone walks toward you, you probably pass one another on the right.

That's how our beliefs work; they operate automatically, just below the surface of awareness. Our beliefs are so commonplace that we rarely recognize them until someone points them out.

Other Managing Beliefs™ that run our lives may include:

"I'm an awful shopper."
"I'm good at remembering names."
"The way he looks at me means he doesn't like me."
"I'm shy."
"Money isn't everything."
"I'm good at selling."
"I fall apart in front of an audience."
"That's just the way I am."
"I can do this."

Misconception 2: *Messing around with beliefs is somehow off-limits, like tinkering with the operating system of your computer.*

## Opening Your Belief Portfolio™

Do you have a 401K or IRA? Those funds are yours, but they are invested in some sort of security instrument, Treasuries, CDs, stocks, or other investment. Do you have the opportunity or right to go into that account and move the funds around? Sure. You might find some limits, but for the most part, you can do what you want with those funds. It's your money.

It's the same with your beliefs. *You* are the one who built them. You are the one responsible for them. Why shouldn't you do what you want with them?

A few years ago, I developed the concept called Belief Investing™. I wanted to capture the idea that each day, one thought at a time, we invest our thoughts, which creates beliefs. We've been doing this "thought investing" all of our lives.

Right now you carry around a bunch of beliefs that represent the thought investments you've made. Your thinking created those beliefs. I call that collection your Belief Portfolio™. It contains the beliefs you've accumulated throughout the years. As in most portfolios, it probably has some good investments, some neutral ones, and some real stinkers.

Why is it, you might ask, that I call beliefs *investments*? Because just like with financial investments, your beliefs enter your portfolio through the thoughts and actions you take. When you see a financial stock you like, you think about it, and then perhaps take action to buy it and put it in your portfolio.

Beliefs operate the same way. We latch on to a way of looking at the world, a way of making meaning of things, and we start thinking and acting as if it were true. We put those thoughts into our mind and operating system as beliefs.

Just like financial investments grow and compound over time, beliefs grow and compound. Good beliefs—ones that are supportive and positive—grow each day and have more effect in your life. Neutral beliefs grow but don't affect your life much at all.

But what about the bad belief investments? Bad beliefs—the ones that can limit and cripple you—also continue to grow. If those beliefs are not removed, the results can blow a hole in your Belief Portfolio™.

Remember that you are the one in control of your Belief Portfolio™ even if you haven't been aware of it. All this time, you've gone through life with a portfolio that, if managed effectively, could make you popular, successful, wealthy, and even famous!

But mismanage that same portfolio, and you could end up alone, a loser, in poverty, and unknown. You may think this is an exaggeration about the power of your beliefs, but if anything, I'm understating their importance.

You can take control of your Belief Portfolio™ and make sure it's filled with the beliefs you want and the beliefs you want for your child.

For stories and examples about the power of beliefs and how changing them can make a difference, go to http://www.BeliefBank.com.

Now we come to the last misconception.

Misconception 3: *Even if you could get in there to examine your beliefs, they're too hard to change, so why bother?*

## You *Can* Change Your Beliefs

You already have experience changing many of your beliefs, but you may not remember it. Let's go back in your mind and identify some of beliefs you used to have, but which have since disappeared from your life.

Did you ever believe in Santa Claus? How about the Easter Bunny? The Tooth Fairy? Monsters under the bed? Well, you say, those are childhood beliefs.

Are those beliefs any different than others you have changed? Maybe there was a time when you thought you'd never be interested in the opposite sex. Maybe you thought that it was difficult to drive a car in traffic or to navigate across a city using a map.

Maybe you thought nothing could get any better than a Walkman, and then the iPod came along. Maybe you thought a cell phone was as good as it could get, and then texting and sending photos came along.

Maybe you believed that you would never live in the city or in the country or in the South or in the East, and then . . .

When you begin to think about it now, you have changed beliefs all through your life and rarely have you noticed how hard or easy it was. So take some time to recognize now how effortless that change has been.

Sure, there are a few beliefs that have been stubborn and resistant to change. Now that you think about it, you may find *even those* beliefs beginning to shift. Once you understand the mechanism behind beliefs and how they operate, you'll know how to take the steps to change your beliefs easily whenever you wish.

For now, if you need to convince yourself that you *can* change your beliefs, you might want to make a list. Draw a line down the middle of a piece of paper. On the left side, make a list of all the past changes of your beliefs that come to your mind. (They *have* started coming to your mind, haven't they?)

Be sure to include all those beliefs that you held as a child that aren't a part of your thinking now.

List all the things you thought you couldn't do and now do with ease.

List all the accomplishments that you thought were out of reach, and yet you've reached them.

On the right side of the page list those beliefs that you have not yet changed and would like to.

As I talk about beliefs and how they form and are maintained, you will begin to see this list differently and wonder about how you can change those beliefs as well.

So, how *do* beliefs form and operate in our lives? In the next chapter, we'll look at how to build a belief. What new beliefs might you want in your portfolio?

## Beliefs to Consider

- Some people think beliefs are some mysterious theological or philosophical stuff that should be left to scholars and theologians.
- Some people think that messing around with beliefs is somehow off-limits, like attempting to change the operating system on your computer.
- Some people think that even if you could get in there to examine your beliefs, that they are too hard to change, so why bother.
- Beliefs are simply the mental programs, the "rules of thumb" we use to run our everyday lives.
- Beliefs allow you to do something, almost on autopilot, while paying attention to something else.
- Our beliefs are so commonplace we rarely recognize them until someone points them out.
- Right now you carry around a bunch of beliefs that represent the investments you've made through your life.
- Your beliefs grow and compound. The good beliefs get stronger, but so do the limiting beliefs.
- You are the one in control of what beliefs go in and what beliefs come out of your Belief Portfolio™.
- You already have the experience of changing many beliefs, but may not remember doing it.
- You have changed beliefs all through your life and rarely have you noticed how hard or easy it was.

- Once you understand the mechanism behind beliefs and how they operate, you'll know how to take the steps to change your beliefs when you wish to.

# CHAPTER 5

# What It Takes to Build a Belief

B eliefs form as we make connections between ideas.
Beliefs develop as we begin to make sense of our
experiences and create our own internal rules to get
along in the world.

Almost from birth, we create these rules. Doing so
is automatic, and, at first, totally unconscious. We try
out things, like crawling or standing up on our own,
and, whatever the result, we make internal rules about
what works and what doesn't. If things continue to
work, we keep doing the same things over and over. If
something doesn't work, we find another way to do it
so we know how to act.

In this way, early human development is much like
what we see in animals:

Stimulus→Response

As we age, things change. We continue to build
an increasingly complex web of equations about what
works and what doesn't, but one day, we *consciously*
begin to make belief statements to explain things. *What*
we think about and *how* we think about things begin to
create our beliefs.

For example, imagine yourself as a child at the beach for the first time. You're in the water when a wave comes along and knocks you over. You frantically kick and paddle, but you feel yourself sinking. You put down your feet and touch bottom, and then come out of the water, sputtering and choking. How do you make sense of what just happened?

The belief you create in that moment could go either way, depending on how you *think* about the event.

Imagine twins going through the same experience. The first twin gets hit by the wave and thinks it was fun. That twin goes, "Wow, what a wave! I got out of that just fine. That was kind of fun. How do I do that again?"

The other twin, meanwhile, thinks the experience was traumatic. "That wave knocked me over. It must be dangerous. I don't want to do that anymore."

Each twin explains the experience in a different way. The first thinks "wave = fun" while the second thinks "wave = danger." Each twin has a different belief.

(Note that the direction a child goes in developing a belief is highly influenced by the presence of a parent and how he or she reacts or responds. From the merest facial expression to an outright declaration, your child *learns from you* how to interpret events. The cumulative effect of each seemingly small intervention is that you help shape your child's meaning of the world. Your influence is immense. And you wield that influence every day whether you recognize it or not.)

Back to the case of the twins: Their different beliefs will enable different behaviors. The twin who believes "wave = fun" runs right back into the water. That twin's motivation is towards the water, towards fun, and into the surf. The other twin believes "wave = danger" and stays away, out of the water, more concerned about security than fun.

Whichever experience you had when you were hit by a wave, you drew a line. Your thinking launched a belief that enables your behaviors and leads to your results.

At what point did you make that decision?

Beliefs begin as provisional statements—temporary ways of thinking to explain what has happened. They are a stab at trying to describe things, and sometimes they can be pretty outrageous.

So if you thought, "That wave knocked me over, so it must be dangerous," that is, in a way, an accurate statement. The wave did knock you over. However, the equation is just a proposal, a temporary statement of a relationship between "wave" and "danger," a statement made with limited experience and very little evidence.

What if you build a belief that is based on faulty information?

You might want to think about whether there have been times when you have done this, when you had an experience and started thinking about it in a particular way. You made a provisional belief statement based on almost no information.

The problem is, as engineers say, there's nothing quite so permanent as a temporary installation. As soon as you made that provisional statement, your mind began to look for evidence to *support* that belief.

Once your mind latched onto the idea, it began moving down one track—to affirm the provisional belief statement. Evidence that disproves the belief has to be pretty compelling to stand a chance of making a difference. Now, in effect, you've made a decision and you may now own this belief.

So if your belief was the result of faulty information—hearsay, rumors, lies, or misunderstandings—there is hope. When you understand that now, you can learn to step away from beliefs based on faulty information. What beliefs come to your mind now that you would like to step away from?

So how do you turn beliefs into the results you want? The next chapter shows how.

## Beliefs to Consider

- Beliefs form as we make connections between ideas.
- Almost from birth we create beliefs—rules or equations. At first, it's automatic and totally unconscious. Eventually we begin *consciously* to make belief statements to explain things.
- Beliefs begin as provisional statements—temporary ways to explain what has happened.
- Belief statements usually start out based on limited experience and very little evidence.
- Once your mind has latched on to an idea, your mind continues down one track—to affirm the provisional belief statement.

# CHAPTER 6

# Turning Beliefs into the Results You Want

What's in the line? Have you ever thought about that?

When you draw a line on a piece of paper, it just sits there. It's not dynamic or active. It's static.

_____

But in life, drawing a line changes things. A line in life kicks off an action by indicating a position, a point of view, and a process.

Drawing a line in life indicates an active division between two choices. It means you have made a decision. You have set a belief in motion.

What happens in your life when you set a belief in motion?

You've probably heard the saying that, "Insanity is doing the same thing over and over again and expecting a different result." Most people understand that this statement refers to a process. Doing something leads to something—behavior leads to a result. If you change your behavior, your results will change.

That is a fact. Changing your behavior *will* change your results.

Changing your behavior often seems hard. Just think of the times you may have tried to keep a New Year's resolution. Something inside wants to prevent us from changing. If you have ever fought against that "something," you know it can be formidable.

What is it?

That "something" is your beliefs—equations, internal programming, mindsets, and inner guidance system—that govern behavior.

Think of it this way: Beliefs are like a gyroscope. Besides being cool toys, gyroscopes are at the heart of many guidance systems—airplanes, ships, missiles, and even that Segway™ personal vehicle. A gyroscope in a guidance system is set to a certain direction. No matter how the vehicle or system is turned, the gyroscope stays aligned to the same position.

In the same way, beliefs keep you pointed in the same direction in spite of changes you try to make in behavior, such as when you've tried keeping a New Year's resolution, or any other time you've tried to change your behavior.

The more you try to turn to a new direction, the more that internal gyroscope works to pull you back to the old course. It's not that there is something wrong with your internal guidance system. In fact, *it is doing exactly what it was programmed to do*—keeping you headed in the direction you set with your beliefs.

In order to really change direction, you need to stop the old rotation of that gyroscope and set it so it points in a new direction. Once you do that, turning in the new direction will be effortless, because your behaviors will be in alignment with your new beliefs.

## What's in the Line?

The line represents a process that I call the Belief-Based Guidance System™: Beliefs enable behaviors, which lead to results.

**Belief-Based Guidance System™**

## Beliefs ➢ Behaviors ➢ Results

The process seems almost too simple, but it is powerful.

Some of my friends have said that the most important thing is to get out there and take action. I couldn't agree more. However, to enable that behavior and kick it into action, you need a compelling belief behind it. If you have trouble taking action on a consistent basis, check out your beliefs. Which of your beliefs inhibits you from taking action?

In many situations, it's important to have beliefs that absolutely compel you to take action. If you find yourself hesitating or pulling back from taking action, ask yourself, "What would I need to believe to make the behavior I want inevitable?"

This is a powerful question. Think of a behavior you would like in your life. What belief would you need, right now, to make your action automatic—even inevitable?

**Belief-Based Guidance System™**

**Beliefs ⟩ Behaviors ⟩ Results**

The process illustrated above goes on inside us all the time. For most of us, it's so commonplace that we don't even recognize when it's happening.

Recognizing it and understanding this process opens a new world of opportunity. Hang with me on this, and I'll show you what I mean.


## How It Worked for Me

Recently, I decided that I wanted to wake up earlier in the morning to write. At various times in the past, I've done this quite successfully. However, this time I experienced some difficulty. The alarm would go off, I'd hit snooze, and I'd be back to sleep almost before I knew it. This wasn't the result I wanted, so I decided to work backwards.

I asked myself what behavior I wanted: to hear the alarm and get up right away.

The next questions I asked myself were, "What belief do I need to do that? What two ideas do I need to associate or link together to enable the behavior?"

I realized that I needed something simple and straightforward, something I could understand while still half asleep! I came up with this statement: "When it goes off, I get right up!"

I knew I'd need practice thinking in a new way, so I gave myself an experience close to the real one by setting the alarm to go off in a few minutes. I lay in bed and waited. While waiting, I repeated the phrase to myself: "When it goes off, I get right up!"

The alarm sounded. I shut it off and got right up out of bed. A few minutes later, I repeated the process.

Throughout the day I did other things to keep thinking in the new way. I kept repeating the phrase to myself and experienced again what it felt like to hear the alarm and get right up. I ran a little video clip in my head—which took only a second—whenever I repeated the phrase.

At first, the mental "video" was the process of hearing the alarm and getting right up. Then I added other things to the picture: I thought about how getting up to write would change other things in my life and get me what I wanted. I added those thoughts and images to the video. I added a picture of how satisfied I would be after getting up to write in the morning. Each video snippet added more motivation and power to my developing belief.

You may be noticing something here. I had an old pattern of thinking that *maintained* the old belief. I had something that I would think to myself, "I'll just sleep a little longer." I had a mental video clip I would run of me shutting off the alarm and going back to sleep.

That video clip included a sense of how good it would feel to sleep a little longer. These thoughts supported and maintained the old belief, so I replaced them with a new set of thoughts that support the new belief.

Since then, just like clockwork, the alarm goes off and I am right up out of bed, no matter what time it is.

Now, you may think this was simple, and almost too simplistic.

That's the point—*it is simple!*

Decide a new direction for your brain—a new way of thinking. Discover what two things you want to link together in a new and powerful way. State the belief you want in the positive. Then draw a line. Say to yourself, "I want *this* rather than *that*. *This* is what I value. *This* is who I will be." Then defend the line you've drawn—visualize yourself actually acting out the new behavior and getting the result you want—in spite of surrounding conditions.

Not every belief changes as easily or quickly as mine did, but this same pattern works for all beliefs. Learn additional techniques to assist in changing your beliefs at http://www.BeliefBank.com.

## How It Can Work for You

You can work the Belief➔Behavior➔Results process backwards just like I did.

What result do you want? What behavior will get you that? Therefore, what do you need to believe to get that behavior?

**Belief-Based Guidance System™**

## Beliefs ⟩ Behaviors ⟩ Results

So, what *result* do you want that you are not currently getting? Go ahead; think of that right now.

Do you have something in mind? Okay, what *behavior* would you need—what would you need to do, what action would you need to take—to get that result?

If you don't know, look to others who have done what you want to do. What behavior did *they* use? What action did *they* take, and how did *they* operate to get that result?

Now, what *belief* do you need to fire off that behavior?

What belief did *they* need to propel them into action? What mindset operates inside of *them* that you can use to fire off the behavior that *you* want?

Identifying the beliefs, behavior, and results of others unlocks a powerful process to produce your own great results:

- Listen to others.
- Notice what beliefs and behaviors work for them.
- Adapt them for your use.

Are you starting to see the enormous potential of this process? You do understand that it is already running inside you, don't you? This process operates without fail; you just need to learn how to use it.

This is what my friend was so excited about when he

said, "It's amazing. Beliefs, behavior, results. It works every time!"

Assume for a moment that in these pages and in the other resources I have for you, that you will learn to use this process. What results will that make possible for you? Just allow yourself to think about that for a moment. What results would you like to create in your life? What dreams that you have forgotten or put on the shelf would you now be ready to go for? What kind of a life could you create for yourself and for your family?

To the point of this book, what could you be doing to combat Belief Bankruptcy™ and build that powerful public virtue in your family and in the country?

Right now, you still may have many questions about beliefs—how they are formed, how they operate in our lives, and how you can change your beliefs.

These questions will be answered later, so for now, just think about what this process means as you teach your children. How powerful will it be when you can show your children how to look at their results, decide what results they want instead, and then help them change their behaviors and beliefs to get the results they want?

What will it mean to your children to see you using this process to change your own life and get results you want?

I have seen the lives of my clients, friends, and family changed in wonderful ways as they take control of this process in their lives. I'll show you how to do it too.

## Language and Beliefs

The three concepts described in the rest of this chapter can revolutionize your life. You may wonder how your language—the words you use and how you use them—affects your beliefs.

We've looked at beliefs and how they develop. We've described how drawing a line sets a belief in motion. We've looked at the line and the process it represents. We've seen how, in real life, the line is dynamic. So let's look at the dynamics of some of the words we'll be using and unpack their real-life meanings.

We'll cover three concepts about language and beliefs: words have power, filling up a word's meaning, and returning words to action.

## Words Have Power

Principle 1: *Words have power.*

Our language patterns—the specific words we use—build our beliefs. The things we say to ourselves determine the beliefs we form, and what we say to others may affect the beliefs they form for themselves.

As we mentally talk to ourselves and try to make sense of an experience, our words not only affect how that belief is formed but how deeply it will impact our subconscious.

Think with me for a few moments as we discuss the subconscious mind and filters.

When we hear things, our conscious mind is aware

of certain things. We identify the context of the conversation. We recognize idioms and slang. We also recognize, to some extent, the intent of the speaker. Our ability to filter this incoming language is part of what could be called our *critical faculty.* This critical faculty enables us to screen out and consider thoughtfully what we hear. It's the ability to be self-reflective and ask, "Is that true?" These things happen in our *conscious* mind.

On the other hand, our *subconscious* mind processes language *literally*—the exact words and their meaning get input into our brains. This happens at the same time as the conscious mind is deciding what was *meant* by what was said.

Most of the time, our two minds work it out. We sort the differences between the literal words and their intended meaning. But sometimes, our critical faculty is temporarily disabled and only the literal words register.

With children, two additional factors are in play. Experts tell us:

- Children understand language long before they can use it. Research about teaching babies sign language has changed our concepts about their abilities. It seems that babies can understand and process language much earlier than previously thought.

- Up until a certain age, children have no filter for language input. What a child hears may go right into the subconscious mind to form a belief. That critical faculty usually is not fully developed until the preteen years.

As I said, even *after* this critical faculty begins operating, certain events—such as severe emotional distress and physical trauma—can temporarily disable this important filter. When that filter is down, a child or adult can take the exact words directly to heart.

You know what I am talking about. When you think about it now, you may remember a time in your own life when you were in a moment of emotional or physical stress and someone's words wounded you. Right now, you can probably even remember those exact words and hear the voice of the person who said them.

Fortunately, you can step back from that event, take a deep breath (do that now; that's right), and see that situation from a different perspective. As you think back on that moment with the current resources you have as an adult, you can change your perception of that event now.

This operation of our conscious and subconscious minds is a fact of life. The important thing to understand is that the words you say matter *because they have power.*

Understanding now that the words you use can have a powerful effect, you may want to reconsider many of the things you habitually say to yourself.

Have you ever been playing a basketball game or maybe golf, and found yourself saying, "I'll never make this shot"? And you found out you were right. The words you say to *yourself* make a difference.

Now that you know how the filters work, you'll also want to be very careful about the words you use with *others,* especially children. From the outside, we can't tell whether filters are operating in a child or even in an adult. If a person's filters are down, the words we say can go right to the heart.

Not long ago, my wife and I were in a department store. My wife overheard the conversation of a mother and her daughter in front of us. The girl wanted her mother's attention and was struggling to get it. The mother, trying to shop, was clearly frustrated. You can probably sympathize with both the daughter and mother.

As both got emotional, the mother raised her voice and said, "You will *never* be happy until you are the center of attention."

Think about the literal meaning those words suggested for the daughter: "You will *never* be happy until you are the center of attention." I don't think the mother ever intended for her words to be taken literally, but words have power.

That situation is rather frightening, but let me assure you, it barely scratches the surface of the ways words can wound children. My hope is that you will become an expert on the words to use to build up your child—powerful, *positive* words. Before we move on to that, one more thing bears mentioning.

Like many people, I grew up in a family that did lots of teasing. As good-natured and light-hearted as teasing is meant to be, it can contain words that genuinely hurt. Young kids (and even adults) don't always have filters running to sort out the literal meaning of the words from the speaker's intent. Even if someone is just kidding and says, "Oh, you'll never get it;

you're too dumb to figure it out," the intent can be misunderstood.

The literal messages are:
- You are dumb.
- You can't figure this out.
- This is about you, personally.
- You'll always be this way.

Be alert to the literal content of your words.

Be careful with teasing. You may understand what is going on, but your child may process those words in a literal, negative way. I won't tell you to cut out all teasing, but do consider how different your family life might be without it. Many careless words are spoken to children, words that can have a powerful, crippling effect.

Fortunately, words can also empower and enable children.

Let's talk for a moment about self-esteem. You may have unconditional love for your child, and I hope you do. That is certainly the foundation of a child's self-esteem and self-regard—your child needs to be sure that he or she is loved.

But after that, much of your child's self-esteem is built on his or her accomplishments. Some parents have the idea that you build self-esteem by telling a child how great he or she is. That may be true to an extent, perhaps, but don't be fooled into thinking that your child can't smoke out empty praise. Give your child real praise. Talk about his or her successes, valiant struggles, and fulfilling victories to build your child's *real* self-esteem.

Remind your child of the past. Use words to help your child replay and relive his or her successes. Use words to remind your child how far he or she has come. Then, use words to point your child toward the future, to think ahead and picture the successes of the school year and of his or her life.

It was a few weeks before Christmas, and my wife and I were shopping in a large department store. Actually, she was shopping, and I was sitting in the "husband recovery area." A woman walked up with her two sons, who were about five and seven years old. As they sat down on a sofa near my chair, I over-heard her say something to them that I found startling: "Remember, good things happen to little gentlemen."

I was blown away by her statement and said, "Excuse me, I couldn't help but overhear. You said, 'Good things happen to little gentlemen.' Is that something you tell your sons all the time?"

The woman looked surprised and said, "Well, I have said things like that to them before, but I think that was the first time I said it in quite that way. Why?"

I went on to explain that I study beliefs and told her that the statement she made was one of the more powerful expressions of beliefs I'd heard from a parent in awhile—it was filled with positive expectation about who they were and could be as "little gentlemen." It was filled with expectation about what the boys could look forward to as a result of their behavior. And all of that was wrapped up in a few simple words that her sons could easily remember.

She seemed surprised at my comments, and she

absolutely beamed at me and at her sons, who were, it must be said, acting exactly like little gentlemen. When I asked if it would be all right to share what she said with others, she readily agreed.

This is a wonderful kind of belief to pass on to children. It *presupposes* that they are good and will behave—in fact, that they *are already* little gentlemen or little ladies. It also communicates that behavior has consequences. It presupposes that, as a result of their behavior, they will experience good things. It points them to the future so they expect and look for good things.

This is a powerful pattern, one which can be applied to more than parenting situations. You might wonder about who you can inspire and encourage by helping them to internalize a powerful belief like this mother's. The words you say to yourself, and to others, make a difference—because words have power.

For more examples and discussion about how words have power and how they affect beliefs, visit my belief website: http://www.BeliefBank.com.

## Filling up a Word's Meaning

Principle 2: *What people **say** to you doesn't necessarily communicate what they **mean**.*

I don't know quite how to say this, but things aren't as they seem. Sometimes when you are in a conversation, you may notice a few things aren't right, but most of us never bother to say anything about it. You see, we all speak the same, but different, language. We use most of the same words, but those words don't have the same meanings.

If you think that I'm exaggerating, try ordering a "jumbo" anything and notice how the meaning of "jumbo" varies from restaurant to restaurant.

Oliver Wendell Holmes captured part of this when he wrote, "A word is not a crystal, transparent and unchanged, it is the skin of a living thought and may vary greatly in color and content according to the circumstances and the time in which it is used."

In many ways, Holmes didn't go far enough, because each of us has our own meanings for the words we use. In a way, it's like we all have our own private language. You'd think that some words would be easy to pin down, but they're not.

How do we begin to make sense of how to communicate when we each have different meanings for words? How did those different meanings come about?

I won't bog you down with technical linguistic stuff about all the ways that words are different. I do want to deal with one of the little known, but commonsense concepts about words, called *surface structure* and *deep structure*. It may sound technical, but it's not!

Think about the first time a young boy meets a dog. The boy sees a little brown dachshund and hears the word "dog," and a little belief is formed. The boy links that particular dachshund with "dog." A few days later, he sees white miniature poodle, and hears the word "dog" again. Suddenly, his concept of "dog" stretches to accommodate the characteristics of this new animal.

It is fortunate that his brain is able to stretch that concept and make those changes, because in the next few weeks he sees more and more dogs. Each time, his concept of what "dog" means changes.

Each time a new dog is added to the concept, the boy gets further and further away from that original direct experience. The boy's concept of the word "dog" gets richer because of all the features and characteristics that have been added. But the word also gets more general and vague, because it no longer means a specific dog. In some ways the word "dog" is more useful, because it can describe more and more of his experience.

If all the dogs in the neighborhood are cute little lap dogs, the boy will develop a concept of a "dog" as a little, friendly animal. When he goes to visit his cousin and she tells him to watch out for the neighbor's dog, he may assume it's the "dog" he knows rather than the Doberman she warned him about.

This example illustrates *surface structure* and *deep structure*.

The *deep* structure in this example is all the underlying experiences that built the boy's concept of "dog." It includes direct experience the boy has with dogs, plus input from stories, books, movies, and so on. All these experiences make up his deep structure of the concept "dog," and fill up the meaning of the word.

Understanding deep structure is why it is important to talk to your children and tell them about your beliefs. Think about what happens when you use the word "honesty." For you it has meaning because of the deep structure you have that supports it—all your direct experiences of telling the truth, being told the truth, or hearing vivid stories about people telling the truth.

You've heard the story about George Washington cutting down the cherry tree and saying "I cannot tell a lie." You know the story about "Honest" Abe Lincoln walking miles to return money to a customer.

When your child first hears the word "honesty" it is an empty word; it isn't yet filled up with experiences to give it meaning. One of your great opportunities as a parent is to fill up words with powerful meaning that will last a lifetime. If you don't help your child fill those words with meaning, someone else will.

What about *surface* structure, the other side of this concept? When someone says, "I'm *honest,* and you can trust me," you're getting a surface structure of the word "honest," just the outer skin of the speaker's meaning for the word. You really don't know the deep structure that person has behind it. The speaker's meaning *might* be close to your deep structure, or it might be very different.

Pastors and youth workers have told me that they sometimes see this effect when they talk about God being our "Father." Some people react negatively to the term.

Subsequent conversation reveals that these people have had a bad, sometimes even violent relationship with their fathers. Their deep structure behind the word "father" has a powerful negative effect on their understanding of God as a Father.

Most of the time, we assume we share the same

deep structure with others. This is a risky assumption, because others have different deep structures behind their words. It's not that a particular deep structure is wrong; it's that everyone has his or her own experience. It's just not safe to assume that we all share the same experience.

What does this mean for you and your children?

Words that are not yet filled with a lot of meaning are susceptible to being twisted or turned by others to mean what they wish. For example, what if a teen has an insufficient meaning of "love"? The word could describe the intense physical attraction that a teen feels, especially when much of the media and culture is more than willing to support that meaning.

Who do you want to be "filling up the meaning" for important words like "love," "honesty," "courage," and "personal responsibility"? You can do this. You can continually recognize and talk about experiences, incidents, and examples in your child's life and behavior that support and fill up the meaning of the word—the deep meaning you want your child to have. You can tell stories of your own experience and point out other examples in books, movies, and on television. Fortunately, pointing out bad behavior can be instructive as well, so the media can actually help you here!

You also may want to adopt and teach your children to use this question: "When you use the word _____, what exactly do you mean by that? Give me an example from your experience."

This question can help you understand the deep structure—the experience and meaning behind the words people use. Demonstrate this question to your children. Teach them how to use it. Practice it at the dinner table. This question prepares your children to discover when words are used deceptively and to unpack the real meanings.

## Returning Words to Actions

Principle 3: *To unlock the full power of words, turn words that are "things" back into actions.*

To take shortcuts with language, we often turn actions or processes into "things"—we turn verbs into nouns. The result is a "thing" that is static or dormant. You may already have gathered this from the description earlier of the difference between drawing a line on paper and a drawing a line in life.

Here are a few more examples:

You might talk about having a *relationship*. That word is really shorthand for all the ways you are *relating* to another person. A relationship is not a "thing"; it is a series of actions, a process.

When we talk about a relationship as a "thing," we can fall into some linguistic traps. For example, we might talk about a relationship being "broken." But how do you fix a "broken relationship"? Do you glue it back together? Do you patch it? How do these ways of fixing broken things apply to a relationship?

Things break, but a relationship is not a "thing." It is an interactive process between two or more people. It's much easier to know how to change a relationship when you start seeing it and describing it as a process. What have you been saying or doing that you could change? How would that affect the way you are relating?

We often talk about our *health.* But what we are really talking about is the way we are *"healthing"*— the process of our physical living. *Wellness* is a noun describing a process, as is *sickness.*

We use these shortcuts so often that we start to *think* of these processes as "things." In order to really understand them, we need to unpack the words and rediscover the original process behind them. When we do that, we begin to realize that many "things" are actually processes, like *peace, love, happiness,* and even *success.*

For a day you might want to recognize all the times you use nouns to describe what are actually processes.

This shortcut of turning actions or processes into nouns is called *nominalization.* (Now you see why I didn't use this word to begin with! It's a big word to describe a simple process.) You can read more about nominalization at http://www.BeliefBank.com.

## Unpacking Beliefs, Morality, Values, and Character

Now, you might be asking, "Why are you talking about this nominalization stuff in the middle of a discussion about beliefs?" It's because belief is a nominalization. Morality, values, and character are nominalizations as well.

A *belief* is the "thing" that we talk about when in the

process of *believing* something. It's not static. We may not use this *believing* consciously every day, but it's there, running in the background. Fortunately, understanding that belief is a *process* (Belief→Behavior→Results) makes it easier to change a belief.

*Morality* is not just a list of stuff that is right or wrong; it's the process of *believing* something about right and wrong in our lives.

Having a *value* is the process of *believing* that one thing is more important to you than another.

In some ways *character* is the most interesting of these words. *Character* is the process of continually and habitually *believing* and acting in accordance with one's beliefs, morality, and values.

Everyone does this. *Character* is the sum of all the Belief→Behavior→Results processes going on in a person. Character inevitably happens as a result of deciding what's right and wrong (morality), deciding what's important (values), and choosing who you will be (character).

What we call *good character* is just as inevitable as *bad character*. It is the result of the beliefs we hold.

We're accustomed to this shortcut of using nouns to describe processes. So, except to point out some particularly important processes, I'll use the shortcuts. Remember, to understand exactly what is happening *and to change it*, you need to turn "things" back into *processes*.

Part Three covers how you begin teaching these concepts to your child.

## Beliefs to Consider

- A line on the page is not dynamic or active. It is static.
- When you draw a line in life, you set a belief in motion. It changes things.
- Drawing a line in life indicates an active division between two choices.
- If you change your behavior, your results will change.
- Beliefs are the equations, the internal programming, the mindsets, the inner guidance system that govern our behavior.
- Beliefs keep you pointed in the same direction in spite of changes you might try to make in your behavior.
- Beliefs enable behaviors, which lead to results.
- Words have power.
- Our language patterns—the specific words we use—build our beliefs.
- Our subconscious minds process language *literally;* the exact words and their meaning get input into our brains.
- Certain events—such as severe emotional distress and physical trauma—can temporarily disable the important critical-faculty filter.
- You may understand what is going on with teasing, but your child may process the words literally.
- Words also can empower and enable children.

- The words you say to yourself and to others make a difference, because words have power.
- Words can have different meanings to different people.
- *Deep structure* describes all the underlying experiences that are behind a person's concept of a word.
- When your child first hears a word, it is an empty word. It is not yet filled up with experiences to give it meaning. If you don't help your child fill up those words with meaning, someone else will.
- It's not safe to assume that we all share the same experience or deep structure.
- When someone uses a word, you are getting the *surface structure*. You really don't know the deep structure that person has behind the word unless you ask.
- To make shortcuts in our language, we often turn processes into nouns. To really understand how these nouns work, you need to turn the *things* back into *processes*.
- A *belief* is the "thing" we talk about when we are in the process of actively *believing* something.
- *Morality* is not just a list of stuff that is right or wrong; it is the process of *believing* something about right and wrong in our lives each day.
- Having a *value* is the process of *believing* that one thing is more important to you than another.
- *Character* is the process of continually and habitually *believing* and acting in accordance with one's beliefs.

Part Three

Discovering Your Role

*If you bungle raising your children,*

*I don't think whatever else you*

*do well matters very much.*

**—Jacqueline Kennedy Onassis**

CHAPTER 7

# Create The Ultimate Legacy™ by Investing in Your Beliefs

You likely realize that you have a great responsibility *to* your children and that your responsibility *for* them ends after a certain age. Children can always reject their parents' beliefs. An heir can choose not to accept an inheritance.

If you don't have a Belief Portfolio™ with useful, empowering beliefs, why would your child want to claim a portfolio like yours? Children are looking for what works in their lives; we all are. If you can show your child that you have beliefs, that they work, and that you work them, then chances are good that your child will embrace those empowering beliefs.

The Biblical story of the Prodigal Son seems to fit here. One day the younger son decided to cash out his part of the inheritance. This kind of request was unheard of in that culture. Since most of his inheritance was in the form of land and livestock, liquidating part of the estate so the younger brother could take his share could not have been easy. But the father did it.

You can read the whole story in Luke 15:11–31, but the part to focus on is the fact that while the younger son may have left home with a share of the father's money, he left behind his father's beliefs. The son proceeded to enjoy a spree of spending and riotous living. Eventually, he blew all the money and ended up with the only job he could find—tending pigs. All he had to eat was the same husks he fed the pigs. It was then that the son had a moment of reassessment and thought: *Even the servants in my father's house have better food than this. I'll go back and work as a servant in my father's house.*

This is a pretty big change in thinking. The son had rejected his father's beliefs and way of life. But now, he not only was willing to go back, but was willing to do so as a servant in the house in which he grew up.

The father saw his son approaching down the road. What he did next was uncharacteristic for the time period. He grabbed the robe around him and ran—*ran* to meet his son. He threw his arms around his son, welcomed him home, and ordered up some new clothes for him and a feast in his honor.

I've always wondered why the son left in the first place. Maybe you have wondered about that too. Every indication is that the father was kind and generous. This story reinforces the idea that you can influence your child's beliefs, but you can never force a child to accept them. Ultimately, we are all responsible for our own choices.

But the son came back. After the big deal he made about leaving, he came back. Why? I think it's because he realized that his father's way of life worked. It wasn't just that there was food at his father's house. The son seemed to know his father well enough to know that he could go home.

His father owned powerful beliefs, and, from what we see in the story, he lived them for his sons to see. Just as with property, you cannot give away beliefs you don't own. You need to invest in and own beliefs before you have any chance of passing them on to your child.

What if all you left your children was money and a few memories? If something happens, and the money goes way, the photos fade, what's left? But you can leave your children something more, something that will last—an inheritance of beliefs, values, and character—an inheritance to last them a lifetime. It's what I call The Ultimate Legacy™. And if you haven't started yet, you can build one right now for your children.

Examining your own Belief Portfolio™ is the starting point. Just as you would look at financial investments to discover what kind of returns can be expected from them, you need to look at your beliefs and consider where they may lead—for both you and your child.

Changing the direction of your life for your kid's sake may sound like some gigantic sacrifice, but consider this: The best thing you can do for your child also happens to be the best thing you can do for yourself. This is what I call the GULP—the Great Ultimate Legacy Paradox™.

Let me say that again: The best thing you can do *for your child* also happens to be the best thing you can do *for yourself.*

Getting your act together and demonstrating a great life to your kid gets you . . . a great life! What more could you want than that?

## Beliefs to Consider

- You have a great responsibility *to* your children.
- You do not have a responsibility *for* them after a certain age.
- Your child can always reject your beliefs.
- Just as with property, you cannot give away beliefs you don't own.
- If you can show your child that you have beliefs, that they work, and that you work them, then chances are good your child will embrace those beliefs.
- The best thing you can do *for your child* happens to be the best thing you can do *for yourself.*

# Chapter 8

# What You Do Speaks So Loud . . .

D o you drive faster than the speed limit with your children in the car? If so, what are you teaching them? How will *they* know to respect lines without showing them that *you* respect lines?

"What you do speaks so loud that I can't hear what you're saying." That's how my father taught me that actions speak louder than words.

How do you get to be heard in your home? Your children will not listen to what you say *until* they believe what they see.

One thing I learned about developing relationships with clients is that you must *win* the right to be heard, and you must *win* that right over and over and over again. You build trust by continuously reselling yourself and proving yourself reliable.

This is no less important with your children and other family members. You need to continually express your love, concern, and devotion to them. Then you have to back those things up with actions. Professing one thing and living another doesn't cut it, especially with the people you live with.

To make sure you are using the opportunity to pass on powerful beliefs to your children, you need to be three things:
- Consistent
- Congruent
- Conversant

## Consistent

Consistency is about being *externally aligned*. That just means *doing what you say you will do, without fail.* Live your beliefs consistently in front of your children, day in and day out.

Don't get me wrong; you don't have to be perfect. You do, however, need to acknowledge and be transparent if inconsistencies do arise. You can still be looking for the right beliefs, behaviors, and results for your life, but you also have to be in there fighting and working for it. Your children will respect you if you are in the game working to improve. They will be close enough to see it.

Allow your children to hear you talk about what you are doing to change your beliefs. Let them see you working at the change, see you doing different things—acting and thinking differently. Keep it simple. No need for complicated explanations and rationalizations.

Being consistent with your beliefs is an important part of your ability to pass those beliefs on to your children.

## Congruent

Congruency is about being *internally aligned*. Being internally aligned simply means that *every part of you matches up with what you say.*

Have you ever had your child come to you excited by something he or she wants to do? Maybe your son wants to become a professional football player, or your daughter wants to become an Olympic gymnast. If you reply with, "That's a great idea," and at the same time smirked, shook your head no, chuckled a little bit, or said it with a sarcastic tone, the incongruence will not go unnoticed. Your child will see and hear that your words don't match your actions or attitude. A moment like that can not only snuff out a dream, but it can cause a child to doubt him or herself.

When two parts don't match up (what you say—is one part, and what you do—is the second part), that is incongruence. Incongruence can happen at the same time, or it can show up over time.

On one day, you might say to your son or daughter, "That's a good idea. You know, you can do that." But then, after some time, the incongruity might begin. When your child takes steps to follow a dream, perhaps you tease or complain about their activities. However the incongruence is displayed, it can undermine the commitment to your beliefs and undermine your child's trust.

Do you see why your children will not listen to what you say until they believe what they see?

But being congruent is even more than that. It affects you as well. When you have a hard time changing beliefs, it is often because you lack congruence in your attempt to make a decision.

On one hand, you say you want to stop a behavior, say stop eating junk food. But at the same time, another part of you is planning where you can hide your emergency pack of Ding-Dongs. You justify the treat by saying it's your last snack fix, but at the same time, you're still thinking ahead to when you could, if needed, get away to make a donut run. You're saying that you're going to quit, but a part of you already knows you don't really mean it.

This is another way in which incongruence is a tip-off to your kids that you aren't serious about your beliefs or that you're unwilling to live them. This sort of internal hypocrisy can turn kids into cynics and skeptics about what adults say.

When you are changing a belief and face internal conflicts that cause incongruence, talk about it with your children. Let them know that sometimes you need to work on parts of yourself as you make a change. Be honest about your struggles; don't try to hide them. By seeing that you face them, your children will be prepared for the struggles that they'll face. Watching how a parent deals with struggles can be a powerful example to a child.

So far, we have covered being consistent and congruent. Doing both of these things wins you the right to be heard. But those two things in and of themselves are not enough. If you have gained the right to be heard, you need to *say* something.

## Conversant

Being conversant is about *talking to your children about your beliefs.*

When I first became interested in this project, I asked people how they talked to their children about beliefs. I can't count how often I was met with blank stares that seemed to say, "No one told me about that part of parenting."

Some said they'd discussed whether some things were right or wrong. Only a few had spent time actually discussing the beliefs they wanted to leave to their children. And some parents *thought* they were talking about their beliefs all the time but weren't.

Are there ever times when you *think* you've been doing something and you discover you haven't been? It happened to me.

"You're not smiling!" he yelled at me.

"Yes, I am," I said. "I'm smiling through the whole song."

I was in the middle of an argument with my new boss. I was just out of college and had joined a rock group. We were expected to be more than just musicians—we were to be entertainers. We had just four weeks at rehearsal camp learning to entertain. A nine-month tour with 15 to 20 shows a week lay ahead of us, and I was in trouble on the first day of rehearsals.

"I know you *think* you are smiling, but you're not," he insisted. "You smile coming out of the applause, you smile when you start the song, but you go back to your old way of performing. This is different than what you've done before. You're here to practice so you can do it the right way all the time."

And so I learned. I learned the difference between what I *thought* I was doing and what I *actually* had to do to be successful on stage.

Some parents are like I was during those early rehearsals: they *think* they're passing on their beliefs by making an occasional mention of what's right and wrong. But to really teach beliefs, you need to be talking about them, repeating them all the time.

Here's a question for you: What advertiser's slogan is, "Just Do It"?

That's right—it's Nike's. How many ads has Nike paid for over the years to tell you and your children to "Just Do It"? How many thousands of impressions have cemented that slogan in your mind and your child's mind? Do you think the slogan has generalized to more contexts than just sports? You've probably used that slogan yourself in a few other contexts. I know I have.

What exactly does "Just Do It" mean anyway? Am I the only one who has noticed that one of the chief spokesmen for Nike—who says "Just Do It"—is Tiger Woods?

How do *your* repetitions of "*Don't* do it" compete with to Nike's thousands of repetitions of "Just Do It"?

As I said earlier, you have a lot of noise to overcome. It's made up of all media, including television, the Internet, texting, movies, video games, and much more that fill up our communication channels. The companies and people behind those media outlets are competing with you for your child's heart and mind. They are serious competition.

And what is the competition after? They want to implant beliefs about what to buy, how to act, what is important in life, even how to live, into our children's minds, and they are challenging your children's beliefs every day.

Don't get me wrong; I'm not implying that this is all done with some evil intent. Mostly, we're talking about marketing people doing their jobs to sell something. They're *very good* at that job.

Make no mistake; the competition knows what they're doing. While you're at work making a living, the competition is at work making plans. For years they've been studying how to get to your children. They are smart and are constantly pushing the boundaries to sell a product. The competition is just going to get more intense as computer and communications technology evolves.

Recently, I had a conversation with a producer from a major network television show. We talked about the competition for a child's mind and heart, and she told me that she was seeing the effects on her family. She was concerned because she knew that the pressure on parents is only going to get worse.

Unfortunately, your children may be no match for the assaults on them. Unless they have some mighty powerful beliefs, they are already outgunned. In fact, it's likely that you are outgunned as well. Right now, you may be no match for the competition in the battle for the hearts and minds of your children.

But you can be. You have a secret weapon—several, actually.

You know each child better than the competition does. You may not recognize that fact yet or know how to use it, but *you* hold the keys to your child's heart. You know his or her preferences, desires, dreams, strengths, and weakness. You know what makes your child laugh and cry.

As he or she has grown, you've had personal experiences with your child that no competitor ever will. Now is the time for you to recognize what you have and use it. Go back to school on your child. Review what you know about him or her.

You are probably concerned about manipulating your children. You are careful about using your influence. You don't want to indoctrinate them. You want them to be free to live and grow to be the individuals they can be.

And this concern is what sets you apart from those competing for the hearts and minds of your children. They're perfectly fine captivating and manipulating your children—body, mind, and spirit. They *want* that kind of control. You don't. They are willing to *fight for it,* and you won't. Why?

The reason is the second big weapon you have—love. You love your children. Your competitors don't. When your children know and understand how much you really love them, that knowledge will change their lives. Show them and tell them of your love each day. That's something no competitor can do.

## Beliefs to Consider

- The first quality you need to pass your beliefs on to your children is consistency, which is about having *external* alignment.
- Consistency means living your beliefs in front of your children day in and day out.
- The second quality, congruence, is *internal* alignment. It means that every part of your *behavior* matches up with what you *say.*
- When what you say doesn't match up with what you do, you have incongruence.
- If you have gained the right to be heard through consistency and congruence, you need to *say* something.
- The third quality you need in communicating beliefs to your children is to be conversant.
- The competition wants to implant beliefs into your children about what to buy, how to act, what is important in life, even how to live, and

they are challenging your children on those fronts every day.

- Your children may be no match for the assaults on them.
- Right now, you may be no match for the competition in the battle for your child's heart and mind.
- You may not recognize the fact yet or know how to use it, but *you* hold the keys to your child's heart.
- The first key is that you know your child's heart better than any competitor will.
- The second key is that you love your child; your competitors don't.

# Chapter 9

# Embracing the Teachable Moment

Has there ever been a time when you needed a child to really listen to you?

When you needed to say, "Do this," or, "Don't do that"? When a child needed to hear, "Walk—don't run—across the street," or, "Don't touch that," or, "No, you can't go out tonight." At times like this, you're telling them what to do. *Telling* is an important part of being a teacher.

Another way of teaching as a parent is teaching by *asking* questions, such as, "What is it you are trying to do?" or, "How did you think of doing it that way?" or, "When you finish this, what will you have?" or, "What other ways can you think of to do that?"

Both *telling* and *asking* are important teaching approaches, not just for parents, but for managers. The *Fifth Discipline Fieldbook,* by Peter Senge and other contributors, discusses management styles that have interesting parallels for parenting.

The authors say that some managers choose the *telling* style. They tell subordinates what to do, give directions, and advocate a specific course of action.

This command-and-control managing style is what they call *advocacy.*

What these managers are missing is what the authors call *inquiry,* which consists of behaviors like observing the employee in action, identifying what seems to be working or not working, and asking questions: What has already been tried? What is the next possible course of action? What result will that action likely have? Some coaches and trainers use this managing and teaching style.

If you've been an employee, you may recognize both styles in your supervisors. Some managers lean heavily on the advocacy style. Their authoritarian approach has several effects on their subordinates. Because they are always told what to do, workers have:

- No incentive to develop their own ideas.
- No opportunity to develop leadership abilities.
- Less feeling of personal accomplishment for a job well-done.

I once coached an executive who exemplified this style. At one point, I interviewed the employees who reported directly to him. Each said that working for him was a demoralizing experience, that they'd never take a risk or propose an initiative, because they'd just be shot down. This experience was so typical, the employees even had a saying: "Why take a risk? Same pay either way."

On the other hand, managers can be too heavy on the inquiry style—asking lots of questions and rarely providing benchmarks and goals. Doing so leaves workers with little sense of direction and mission.

So there are downsides of each style. Here's the upside:

The best summary I've ever heard of the role of manager came from a CEO I worked with who said that managers needed to be "loving and requiring." He explained that "loving" meant valuing, respecting, supporting, and affirming his people. "Requiring" was about setting high standards, holding high expectations, and demanding excellence from his people.

"Loving and requiring" sounds like the kind of balance parents need with their children.

## Utilization

Have you ever been in a situation where things went wrong—or at least something unexpected happened—but someone was able to turn the experience around and make it successful after all?

When my nephew Andy was very little, he was used to running around the house barefoot. One day he ran into a table leg, stubbing his big toe. He howled in pain and came over to show me the damage.

I said, "Ouch, that looks really bad. Do you think we need to call a tow truck?"

Andy stopped, thought a moment, and then started laughing. The bruised toe was forgotten, but he has always remembered my quip about calling a tow truck.

Milton Erickson, physician and hypnotherapist, contracted polio as a child. Though the disease did not kill him, he spent nearly a year in an iron lung to assist his breathing. Flat on his back, with a mirror above him so he had at least some view of his surroundings, Milton watched what little he could and listened to his large family. Unable to see the faces of family members, he learned to recognize subtle changes in emotion by listening to their voices. After years of physical rehabilitation, Milton became a doctor. As a doctor, and later as a psychiatrist, he put to use his ability to recognize small emotional shifts with his patients.

I think I first heard about the idea of "utilization" when reading about Milton Erickson. He purposely incorporated whatever happened in a session into his work. If there was an interruption, he'd comment on it and work it into what he was saying. If a dog barked outside the office, Dr. Erickson mentioned it and found a way to use that as part of what he was doing with the patient. If a patient suddenly began to cry, he used that fact in the session.

Erickson's daughter tells of when she was just a little girl and fell, cutting her head. Even though it wasn't a deep cut, there was lots of blood, which scared her. Her father took her hand and told her that while someone was taking care of that little cut, she had a decision to make. He opened her hand, palm up, and placed a nickel and a dime there.

He pointed to them and said that when the cut was fixed up, she would need to choose which coin she wanted. The nickel was the bigger coin. But the dime was worth more—it would buy more candy. While the little girl was occupied with her decision, someone else was able to take care of the cut.

What is important about this story? Dr. Erickson recognized a moment, an instant that could have had a potentially powerful negative effect on his daughter, and took the opportunity to acknowledge that cut and reassure her that it would be fixed. But then he set her to thinking about something else—trying to solve a different problem.

Not long ago, an acquaintance named John told me about an experience with his son.

John used to put his son to bed every night. One night when his son was about eight years old, John had put in a particularly busy day and still had work to finish that night. As he went in to tuck his son in, the boy began to tell about what happened at the playground that day. He was excited, unfocused, and rambling as only an eight-year-old can be. John listened for awhile, and then, getting impatient, made a hurry-up motion with his hand.

His son stopped. He didn't say another word. Instead, he pulled up the covers and turned away. John tried to get him to talk again, to no avail. His son wasn't going to say another thing. John realized what he'd done, how he'd hurt his son. Quietly, he lay on the floor next to his son's bed. Nothing happened. His son didn't say a thing. John lay there until his son fell asleep.

The next night, John did the same thing. He put his son in bed, tucked him in, and lay on the floor beside the bed. Once again, his son didn't say a word. Three nights this went on, and on the fourth, his son spoke again. The two had a good conversation. And they did the same every night after that, until his son went away to college, John lying on the floor and talking with his son.

Today, John's son is an adult, and they still have a wonderful relationship that began the night John took a difficult situation and turned it into a teaching moment for both of them.

What do these stories have in common? In each case, someone remained in the moment to experience and use that moment for a child.

You, too, can do this. You can be in the moment and recognize an opportunity for you and your child. You can turn accidents and problems into teachable moments by how you react. You still need to hold your child accountable for his or her actions. But you can move to *inquiry* mode and ask, "I wonder why that happened?" rather than go to the *advocacy* mode by demanding, "Why did you do that?"

These teachable moments come when you can ask your child what he or she thinks. These moments come when helping your child figure things out for him- or herself. Maybe you need to be the expert at work, but at home, you can be an adventurer. As you ask questions and lead your child on a treasure hunt for what's right, what's of value, and what constitutes good character, you teach your child inquiry, self-reliance, and self-confidence.

You can do this. Ironically, you can prepare to be spontaneous. You can prepare yourself now for the unexpected and be ready to utilize those teachable moments.

Ask yourself these questions:
- What would I need to believe to be in the moment?
- What would I need to believe to be a more *loving and requiring* parent?
- How can I use whatever comes so that I *learn and grow?*
- How can I use whatever comes for *building the relationship* with my child?
- How can I use whatever comes *to teach* my child?
- How can I *use the moment* to draw a line?

## Beliefs to Consider

- Both *telling* and *asking* are important styles for parents.
- *Advocacy* is a command-and-control style of *telling* someone what to do.
- *Inquiry* is a style of observing others in action, identifying what seems to be working or not working, and *asking questions* about what has already been tried, what a possible course of action might be, and what effect that action is likely to result in.
- Managers need both *advocacy* and *inquiry* styles—and so do parents.
- Parents need to be both *loving* and *requiring* with their children.
- *Utilization* is incorporating whatever happens into what you say and do in the moment.

- By asking questions you can help your child figure things out for him- or herself.
- You can be in the moment and recognize an opportunity for you and your child.
- You can turn accidents and problems into teachable moments by how you react.

Part Four

---

# Drawing The
# Three Life Lines™

*Authentic values are those by which a*

*life can be lived, which can form a people*

*that produce great deeds and thoughts.*

**—Allan Bloom**

# The Three Life Lines™

Now we come to what prompted me to write this book. For a long time, I've thought about whether there was a simple set of organizing principles that parents could use to teach beliefs to their children.

I realized those principles would need to be:
- Simple enough to be used with young children.
- Profound enough to use for the rest of one's life.

The principles also needed to help one distinguish truth on three different levels:
- **Morality:** What is ultimate truth—right and wrong?
- **Values:** What is *my* truth—how do I value the things in my life?
- **Character:** How do I incorporate that truth into my life? (Literally—how do I get that truth into my body and being?)

Then one day, the image of three lines popped into my head. As I began to share them with people, the three lines seemed to have a profound effect.

For a long time, I didn't know what to call the lines as a group, but then I began to realize that their effect in a person's life was to build one's inner strength—they fortify one's heart.

I hope you, too, will find them to be life lines for you and your child.

## A Note about The Three Life Lines™

In the illustrations for each of the lines, I have used the initial letter of each, such as M for the Morality Line. I encourage you to write and talk about them in the same way, especially with young children. You don't need to get into a big discussion of the names of the lines and what they mean for the lines to have an impact. Simply concentrate on answering the questions associated with each line.

When your child is older and ready to learn about morality, for example, you can approach it this way: "You may have wondered what the M stands for. Each time we have used this line, you've made decisions—about what is right or wrong. That's what morality is. You've already been making judgments about morality."

# CHAPTER 10

# Draw the Line at Right and Wrong

A line exists between right and wrong. Although we may argue and discuss where exactly that line is, rarely does someone dispute that the line exists. (Occasionally questions arise about "gray" areas. As we'll see, they arise most often when moral and value questions become confused.)

So, start by drawing a line.

**What is right, and what is wrong?**

Right . . .

**M** _____

Wrong . . .

The question that goes with the Morality Line is: "What is right, and what is wrong?"

When you look at situations in your life, sort them out by writing the RIGHT thing above the line and the WRONG thing below the line.

99

As an adult, this may seem elementary. Do it anyhow, and talk with your child about it. Your child may see you doing things, but may not identify them as necessarily *right* without your explanation. You need to show *and* tell your child what is right and what is wrong.

For that matter, it's not a bad idea for adults to review these choices as well, for you to think seriously about what things are morally right and wrong. It's easy to let the line slip on some of the small things, to say that *this* doesn't really matter, or it's just this once.

The problem: It *does* matter.

Find ways to consistently and congruently reexamine your beliefs, especially about issues of morality. If something is right or wrong, call it what it is. Decide, draw, and defend the line.

What kinds of "small things" am I talking about?

- Breaking the speed limit
- Gossiping about others
- Telling "white" lies because they are convenient
- Losing your temper and going into a rage
- Carrying on a grudge with a neighbor

We each have our own list of questionable things—things which are probably wrong, but are easy to justify in the moment. These things can have a corrosive effect on us and, ultimately, on our children.

Let me say that I claim no particular standing to be able to talk about morality. I'm reminded of the 70s-era bumper sticker, "I'm not perfect, just forgiven." I am consistently made aware of my personal shortcomings. But not always being able to live up to a standard of morality doesn't mean we shouldn't draw a bright line between right and wrong.

Letting these small moral decisions slip by can result in at least three problems.

First, there is the *internal* problem. Each decision we make changes us. The change may be small and almost imperceptible, but, as a friend of mine says, "Small commitments lead to big commitments." Each decision we make redraws the line in our own minds and hearts. It is these seemingly unimportant decisions by which we shape our beliefs, values, and character.

C.S. Lewis wrote, "Every time you make a choice, you are turning the central part of you, the part of you that chooses, into something a little bit different from what it was before and taking your life as a whole, with all your innumerable choices, all your life long you are slowly turning into a creature that's in harmony with God and with other creatures and with itself—or else into one that is in a state of war and hatred with God."

If that's too religious for you, then consider Eleanor Roosevelt's words: "One's philosophy is not best expressed in words; it is expressed in the choices one makes. In the long run, we shape our lives and we shape ourselves. The process never ends until we die. And, the choices we make are ultimately our own responsibility."

Second, there is the *external* problem. When we let the line slip or ignore it, we are changing the meaning of the line.

Let me explain it this way. Each time you let the line slip, it's like putting a drop of black paint in a bucket of white paint. For a while, you may not notice any change. But soon, if you keep looking at that bucket of white paint as your standard, *white* will have lost its meaning. The clear dividing line between black and white is now somewhere between black and gray, and your original standard is meaningless.

Third, there is the *relational* problem. What does your child do with your inconsistency—with the change in your interpretation of the line? When you tell your child to follow all the rules but you break the speed limit, what does your child learn?

Back in Psychology 101, I ran the usual experiments with white mice. The goal is to teach a mouse to press a lever for food. Every time the mouse comes even *near* the lever, it gets some food. Eventually if it *touches* the lever it gets food. With a hungry mouse and a little bit of time, it was easy to train the mouse to *press* the lever for food.

Next, you extinguish the behavior. You give no food when the trained mouse presses the lever. The mouse gets more and more agitated, but eventually when no food comes from pressing the lever, the mouse stops doing it.

Finally, you provide inconsistent reinforcement—sometimes the mouse gets food when it presses the lever, and other times it doesn't. Very quickly, the mouse becomes unteachable and unruly. The inconsistency of reinforcement causes the mouse to quit learning.

Kids are more resilient than mice, but when they get inconsistent reinforcement, teaching them about right and wrong and expecting them to sort out the two becomes difficult.

## What to Say about Morality?

Not only will you want to teach your child that some things are right and wrong, but, at the right age, you will also want to teach about the idea of morality. This list will can get you started in thinking about what to say and how to talk to your child about right and wrong.

- Talk about how certain things are right and certain things are wrong. You may want to physically draw the line on paper to provide a right thing to do for every wrong thing you identify.
- Talk about where these right and wrong things come from. If you believe God said they are right or wrong, cite that authority. If you believe the authority comes from tradition or government action, describe that.
- Talk about the consequences of crossing these lines—the internal and external consequences as well as those on the heart.
- Talk about your experience crossing lines and what it might have cost you.
- Talk about what it may take to repair that damage.

## Beliefs to Consider

- Sort things on the Morality Line by writing the RIGHT thing above the line and the WRONG thing below the line.

- The question that goes with the M line is, "What is right, and what is wrong?"
- Small commitments lead to big commitments.
- Whether something is right or wrong, call it that. Decide, draw, and defend the line.

CHAPTER 11

# Putting Values on the Line

Each of us has values that are important to us—
things that are of worth to us.

Draw the Values Line:

**Which is more important to me?**

CONTEXT:

Higher
Value . . .

**V** ⟍_____✍

Lower
Value . . .

For any given context, write the HIGHER VALUE
thing above the line and the LOWER VALUE thing
below the line. The question for this line is, "Which is
more important to me?"

We all value things. Operating in the world would
be easy if we all had the same values, but we all have

105

our own ideas of what is of worth. You may think that a new car is important, but your spouse may prefer to have the house painted. You may think that the most important thing in a relationship is having fun and being friends, while your partner thinks that commitment is more important. None of these choices are necessarily right or wrong. They are simply different points of view. People are different, and they value different things.

It's also important to understand that values can be contextual, where the situation, or context, is important in deciding on the value. For example, when you go out to grab some lunch, you may value speedy service over attention to detail. However, when you go out for a special dinner, you prefer attention to detail over speedy service.

**Which is more important to me?**

CONTEXT:
*At lunch*

Higher
Value . . .

V    *Speedy service*
     —————————————————
     *Attention to detail*

Lower
Value . . .

**Which is more important to me?**

CONTEXT:

*At a special dinner*

Higher
Value . . .

V   *Attention to detail*
   _____
   *Speedy service*

Lower
Value . . .

The value depends on the context. Remember to specify what context you are talking about as you figure out your values.

## Why Values Matter

The discussion above would lead one to conclude that values are not only contextual, but that they could be called "personal preferences."

Many of the conflicts we face occur when someone elevates a personal preference to the level of morality and tries to make this *preference* an issue of right and wrong for everyone.

For example, it's one thing to say that I have looked at the options and have decided that I value eating a vegetarian diet. I feel better and seem to be healthier without eating meat. That's a personal preference. It is quite another thing to say that *everyone* should be vegetarian. If I say that eating vegetarian is a moral decision and attempt to force my personal decision on others, that act violates their personal freedom.

I began with the Morality Line and not the Values Line for a reason. Morality should influence values and not the other way around.

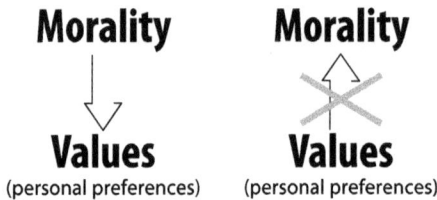

**Morality**　　**Morality**

**Values**　　**Values**
(personal preferences)　(personal preferences)

We just talked about the difficulties of elevating personal preferences (values) to the status of moral standards. It is, however, appropriate to take moral standards and apply them to the Values Line.

For example, telling the truth is an issue of morality, *and* it also is an important value for most people. In fact, as you think about it, you may want to ask what moral standards you want to show up in your values. It can be a useful lesson for your child to see and hear from you how your moral standards play out in your values.

Values are important because our happiness or fulfillment depends on whether we are getting what is important to us. You may have heard of someone who left a good job because they weren't finding satisfaction in it. They valued satisfaction over the security of their previous job. Then there are people who stay in jobs they don't like year after year because they value security over satisfaction.

Our values drive and motivate us. You can help your children find fulfillment in their lives by discovering their beliefs about what is important and then by helping them get those things.

## What to Say about Values?

Here is a list of the kinds of things you might want to communicate to your child about values. This is not meant to be a complete list, but an invitation to think about what kinds of things you can talk about together.

- Think about what is important to you—what you value.
- Be aware of what things you value more than others—how you rank your values. Do this by comparing one value to another until you know what is *really* important to you.
- Distinguish between *moral* standards and *value* decisions. Ask, "Is it a matter of right and wrong (morality), or is it a matter of personal preference *for me* (values)?"
- Understand that other people value things differently—and that's okay.
- You can respect the values of others without agreeing with them.
- You have a right to your values and to talking to others about your values. You do *not* have the

right to impose your values on others. Others do not have the right to impose their values on you.
- We choose to do or not do certain things because we hold certain values as a family.
- You can decide, draw, and defend lines about your values.

## Beliefs to Consider

- To sort out your values with the Values Line, write the HIGHER VALUE thing above the line and the LOWER VALUE thing below the line.
- The question for the Values Line is, "Which is more important to me?"
- Values may differ according to context, so specify the context with the values you are considering.
- We all have our own ideas of what is of worth.
- Value choices are not necessarily right or wrong. They're just different points of view.
- People are different, and they value different things.
- Sometimes a value—a personal preference—can get promoted to being seen as a moral choice. This occurs when someone wants his or her preference to be mandated for everyone.

# CHAPTER 12

# Decide Who You Choose to Be

Drawing the Character Line is about choosing who you will become.

**Who do I choose to be?**

Who I
Choose
to Be . . .

C _____

Who I
Used
to Be . . .

Below the line, write who you are now. Above the line, write who you choose to be.

Earlier we discussed beliefs and their importance. The Character Line is the personally applied part of beliefs, where you ask yourself, "What beliefs no longer serve me well?" and, "What beliefs do I want instead?"

The first two lines we looked at—the Morality Line and the Values Line—are analytic. They are investigative. Drawing those lines will help you clarify and sharpen your thinking.

The third line is a great deal more than that. Yes, it is investigative, because you will need to think about and write down who you are now. But writing down who you will *become* is a profoundly transformative act.

When you make a decision, when you say, "This is who I *choose* to be," and write it down, it moves the old "you" into the "Used to Be" category. You are making a powerful change. You are saying "NO" to what you write below the line and "YES" to what you write above it.

In a very real way, this line could also be called the *decision* line, because character and choosing are about making decisions—deciding once and for all who you will be.

You may be asking, "What's all this *once and for all* stuff? If I make a decision that I don't like, I can always change it."

True, but that misses the point of what "decision" means. "Decision" comes from the same root word as "incision" meaning to "cut into." "Decision" literally means to "cut off" any other possibilities.

A friend told me about a man known for being indecisive. He was really good at seeing both sides of an issue and often found it difficult to choose a course. One day a big question came up. For weeks the man walked around talking to himself about the issue, weighing one side and then the other. Just as his family got tired of hearing him talk about it, he showed up at a family gathering and announced emphatically, "I have decided." His family breathed a sigh of relief, until he continued, "I'm either going to do it, or I'm not!"

That's the problem some people have with their decision making: they don't draw a firm line and say, "This is it. *This* is who I will be and what I will do." When they don't draw a firm line, they are saying, in effect, "I'll do this, but I'll leave open the possibility of doing something else." They don't cut off other possibilities.

Granted, some decisions may require time. You may decide that you want to be more outgoing and friendly and want to try that for awhile to see how it works. In matters like this, a tryout is appropriate to help you decide just exactly who you should be in each situation. But all these style considerations are still built around a core of solid beliefs about how to value and treat other people.

We talked earlier about congruence and incongruence. Sometimes, incongruence comes from not making a real decision. If you have been waffling, now is the time to make a decision. You can delude yourself that you are making a decision, or you can actually decide and cut off the other alternatives. The choice is up to you. At least recognize how you have been sabotaging your effort to change by keeping open a couple of emergency exits.

Maintaining congruence is important not only because of what it does to you, but because of what it does to your child. What does your child learn when seeing you "make a decision" and then abandon it at the first sign of trouble or difficulty? What will your child do at the first sign of trouble or difficulty?

Keep your word. Keep your word with your children. And keep your word with yourself. If you have acted in ways that undermine your character, you can begin rebuilding it. You can draw new lines and cut off other options so that your "yes" means "yes' and your "no" means "no."


## Choosing a Life of Good Character

What do you write above your Character Line? Who do you choose to be?

Start by looking at what is already working in your life. What choices have you made that created the results you wanted? What thoughts and beliefs did you invest in?

Next, you look at places in your life where you *don't* like the results. As described earlier, beliefs enable behaviors, which lead to results. If you don't like the results you're getting, work backwards to find the behaviors and beliefs that made your current result possible. Change the beliefs and behaviors, and you'll change the results.

Drawing a line about who you will be merely marks the beginning of change. At times you may be called upon to defend the line that marks who you are. You may need to add additional supporting beliefs to underpin your declaration.

A few years ago I met Werner at a conference. The

leader of the conference, who knew Werner, asked him to tell about his achievements. Werner told us how, even though he was at an age when most would be thinking of retiring, he'd decided to climb the highest mountain on every continent. He began training, and over the years he systematically checked each of the world's tallest mountains off his list except for one. It was time for Mt. Everest.

He told the conference attendees how he was able to join an expedition and became the oldest person to ever climb Mt. Everest. (That record has since been broken, but Werner says he's going back to reclaim the record someday.)

While his presentation was interesting, it was what I learned from him at lunch one day that impacted me most. Four or five of us sat around the table. I asked Werner what it was like when he knew the team would be making that last push up to the summit from the base camp. He said that most people don't really understand that part of the climb. Most people think it's just, "Get to the base camp and wait for the right weather for the push to the top."

Instead, Werner said that because one needs to become acclimated to the altitude, climbers move back and forth between the upper and lower base camps. Even well-conditioned climbers can't stay at the upper base too long without starting to lose fitness. The team spent a few days at the lower camp, went to the upper camp for a few days, then went back down to the lower camp to rest up. This back-and-forth conditioning process continued for a few *weeks* so the climbers could build up the strength and endurance they'd need to reach the summit.

Werner said that the trip to the top was amazing. It's the moments at the summit that most people want to hear about. But it's the *preparation* that made it all possible.

Years ago, another climber, Sir Edmund Hillary, gave a speech in London after his initial, failed, attempt to reach the summit at Mt. Everest. A photograph of Mt. Everest was projected on a screen behind him. As he spoke, emotion was evident in his voice. At one point, Hillary turned to the picture of the mountain and said, "Everest, you have beaten me. But it's not finished, because you cannot grow any larger, and I can. I will defeat you."

A few years later, Sir Edmund Hillary did just that. And many years later, Werner did it. In each case, a decision was made to achieve the goal, and all the failures and struggles were part of the process. Werner said that without the struggles and the trips back and forth between base camps, he'd never have made it to the summit. He had to be willing to fall back, to retreat, to advance and retreat, and advance again, while he grew equal to the task.

Right now, if you have a broken resolution, do you see it as the end, or just another step in your own success? Are you willing to keep at the process, letting yourself grow in the meantime, keeping your eyes on the result? What would you need to believe to keep on in spite of failure? What would you need to believe to conquer your personal Mt. Everest?

Developing character starts with a decision, but it is a continual process of consistently drawing the line and defending it.

## What to Say about Character?

How do you teach your children to build a life of character? What questions can you ask and what things can you say to help them choose who they want to be?

- You can choose who you want to be.
- The thoughts and beliefs you build every day will build you into the person you will ultimately become.
- Who do you want to be? What kind of a person?
- Who do you admire? What makes that person who they are? What qualities? What beliefs?
- What beliefs do you need to build to make that possible?
- What would you need to believe to be the person you would like to become?
- We do or do not do certain things because that is who we *choose* to be.

## Beliefs to Consider

- The Character Line is about *choosing* who you will become. Above the line you write who you choose to be. Below the line you write who you were before you chose differently.

- This line is about saying, "This is who I *choose* to be."
- You are saying "NO" to what you write below the line and "YES" to what you write above it.
- *Decision* literally means to "cut off" any other possibilities.
- Incongruence can come from not making a real decision.
- Understand that drawing a line about who you will be just marks the beginning of change.
- Developing character starts with a decision, but it is a process of consistently drawing the line and defending it.

# CHAPTER 13

# Resetting the Boundaries for Yourself, Your Children, and the Nation

As you near the end of this book, let's review what we've covered.

We've talked about beliefs, boundaries, and lines, and the process that starts once you draw or recognize a line.

We've established that:

Beliefs enable behaviors, which lead to results.

**Belief-Based Guidance System™**

### Beliefs ⟩ Behaviors ⟩ Results

From the outset, I said that my vision for this book, my result, is to inspire and equip you to build powerful, positive, life-changing beliefs that set boundaries for you and your children and restore boundaries for the nation.

Along the way, I have provided a framework of

beliefs that, if you choose to embrace them, will enable you to develop the behaviors you need to get the results you want.

I have talked about some general behaviors and a few specific ones. Part of your task now is to build beliefs and behaviors that:

- Reflect who you are.
- Reflect your situation—whether you have a spouse to help you on this process or whether you are doing it by yourself.
- Reflect your personality and talents.
- Reflect the beliefs and values you really want to pass on to your child.

Of course, this book doesn't include all the beliefs you'll ever need. I encourage you to do some reading. Study to see if there are some areas of belief you need to enhance. The framework of beliefs presented here gives you a start to find and build additional beliefs.

Each chapter in this book ends with a list of beliefs.

- Most are beliefs you likely hold already.
- Many are beliefs that you will find easy to embrace with just a little thought.
- Some are beliefs that put ideas together in ways that may be new and different for you.
- A few are beliefs that may have knocked you back on your heels, making you say, "Ah-ha!" Those beliefs will cause you to have a massive transformation of your life over time.

The question is, which beliefs fit into which of the categories above? Right now you can start sorting them out in your mind.

Throughout, I've emphasized this one belief:

*Decide, draw, and defend your own boundaries, or someone else will do it for you.*

That's the process that each of us will take in drawing lines for ourselves. But there is a slightly different process in passing those beliefs on to your children. To do that, you need to *choose, change,* and *convey.*


## Choose

You need to choose beliefs that work for you—beliefs that motivate and enable the behaviors and results you want in your life.

You already may have some wonderful beliefs in your portfolio that are working in your life. Cherish those beliefs. Tell your children often how important those beliefs are, how you got them, and what those beliefs can do for them.

At the same time, be aware of beliefs that may be limiting you, diminishing your value, and holding you back from the greatness for which you were created.

No one can dictate to you the beliefs you use to run your life.

Victor Frankl, a psychiatrist and survivor of the Auschwitz prison camp in World War II, wrote about this. He describes that in the midst of all the horror around them, some prisoners refused to give in to hopelessness. In *Man's Search for Meaning,* he wrote, "Everything can be taken from a man or woman but one thing: the last of the human freedoms—the ability to choose one's attitude in a given set of circumstances, to choose one's own way."

With this power to choose comes a responsibility. The beliefs you choose affect your behaviors and results, and those affect your child. Remember, you can only give away what you own. So choose wisely the beliefs you want in your life.

## Change

Do you have beliefs you need to get rid of? What limiting beliefs no longer work for you? What empowering beliefs would you like to add? What beliefs do you need to change for your sake? What beliefs do you need to change for your child's sake? What would you need to believe to make those changes now?

Throughout much of this book, when we've talked about "drawing the line," it's been about setting a boundary in the external world. But drawing the line also is about looking at your internal world and asking, "What will I no longer accept? Where do I need to draw the line in my own life?"

For example, you might say, "I am no longer willing to accept myself as a cynic. I will look for the best in others, encourage the best in others, and expect the best from myself." Draw a line about what thoughts you allow into your mind and heart. Soon you'll recognize a difference in your life.

Change is the process of making decisions—drawing lines—to cut off beliefs and behaviors that are no longer useful, appropriate, and fitting for your life and the results you want.

Find more resources and techniques to help you choose and change your beliefs at the Belief Investing™ website, http://www.BeliefBank.com.


## Convey

Once you are on your way to shaping up your beliefs, convey them to your child.

You already have been transmitting beliefs to your child for his or her entire life. Now you can choose to teach beliefs on purpose.

How do you do that? As part of loving your children, talk to them about your beliefs and the beliefs they're developing.

A model for this is found in the Bible. Though I think it is a powerful spiritual statement, for now, just think about the *process* that is outlined in Chapter 6 of Deuteronomy.

As we pick up the narrative, God has just told Israel that of all the peoples and nations, He has chosen them and will make a great nation of them. Because of His love for them, He will make a covenant with them, a promise that will last for all time.

God then tells Israel that He is drawing some lines. These lines, designed to keep the Israelites on the right path, are the Ten Commandments. And then God gave another, even more important, commandment that follows the ten.

The people of Israel are told to "Love the Lord your God with all your heart, with all your soul, and with all your strength."

(As an aside, notice that the people of Israel are asked to be congruent in their love for God so that all of their being is in alignment with that love.)

God then follows those commands with these instructions found in Deuteronomy 6:6–9:

"These commandments that I give you today are to be upon your hearts. Impress them on your children. Talk about them when you sit at home and when you walk along the road, when you lie down and when you get up. Tie them as symbols on your hands and bind them on your foreheads. Write them on the doorframes of your houses and on your gates."

Let's look at the pattern:
- First, affirm and show love.
- Second, draw the line about right and wrong.
- Third, point to the larger, more important thing (in this example, loving God).
- Fourth, talk about the commandments (or your beliefs)—all the time.

Parents need to talk about beliefs—talk about them at home and away from home, at all times of the day. Parents are to write them down and have them around the house. This talk about beliefs is to be woven into all of a family's life together.

What would it be like to put this into practice in your home? What can you do to make conversations about beliefs a natural part of your life together—day in and day out?

It might be a challenge to start this at home with a couple teenagers or even pre-teens in the house. It's probably easier for parents to start when their children are young. But when you win the "right to be heard" with love, you can have success discussing beliefs with children of any age. When your children believe what they see, they will begin to listen to what you say.

You can do this. You have a lot more influence on your children than you may think. Your children want to look up to you and be proud of you. Step up and be a hero in your home. Download my free Special Report, *7 Ways to be a Hero in Your Home,* at http://www.HeroInYourHome.com.

## One Last Thing: Core Beliefs

Chapter 4 talked about some of the misconceptions about beliefs. Let's return to the first misconception. Remember, some people think beliefs are mysterious theological or philosophical stuff that should be left to theologians and scholars. We talked about Managing Beliefs™, the smaller beliefs that we use to run our lives.

Starting the discussion with small beliefs was useful, because it is easy to see how they operate. Now it *is* time to talk about those big theological and philosophical beliefs.

As you've read and thought about beliefs and how they operate, you may have figured out that your big beliefs—Core Beliefs—are going to have some pretty big effects on your behaviors and results.

The introduction to Part 4 lists principles to help distinguish truth on three different levels:

- **Morality:** What is ultimate truth—right and wrong?
- **Values:** What is *my* truth—how do I value things in my life?
- **Character:** How do I incorporate that truth into my life? (Literally—how do I get that truth into my body and being?)

Ultimately there is another level of truth to deal with, and that is, "Who is the author of the lines?" If these lines are to have meaning, if we are going to trust those lines, we need to know who drew them.

It's not just a question of knowing the identity of the author, but of trusting the *character* of that author.

An art scholar who studies a particular artist begins to know the touch and sensibility of that artist. Every color, every line, comes alive to the scholar. The heart of the artist becomes plain to the scholar, so much so, that each painting can be positively identified as the work of the master.

If you believe, as I do, that there is a God who established our rights, who gave us lines and boundaries, you can see His character in His works. I encourage you to look for Him and discover the love that is behind the lines.

## A Note from the Author

Throughout this book I've described many beliefs that enable you to teach beliefs to your children, and I've avoided giving specific beliefs for you or for you to pass on. It's your job to choose those beliefs. However, I'd like you to carefully consider what I'm about to say.

I believe that the most powerful gift you can give your children is belief and trust in a personal, loving God who really cares about them. You can open the door to their understanding of that kind of spiritual relationship by your unconditional love for your children. However imperfect human love may be, your love *will* help them fill up the meaning of a Heavenly Father who loves and cares for them.

There are two reasons why I'm taking this space to talk about the importance of faith in God. First, there is solid evidence that faith in God affects one's survival in the world.

In his book *The Survivor's Club,* Ben Sherwood, tells about the work of Dr. Harold G. Koenig of Duke University Medical Center. Dr. Koenig is a leader in psychoneuroimmunology, the study of how the mind influences health. Sherwood writes:

"Almost anything is possible, Dr. Koenig says, when you believe that God loves you, that He has a plan for your life, that He will never leave you alone and will give you strength to handle your hardships. Faith and religion, he says, empower you with 'the kind of strength that nothing else that I've ever seen can give.'"

I highly recommend *The Survivor's Club* as a source of many powerful beliefs to pass on to your children.

Second, my own parents demonstrated the kind of love that enabled me to put my trust in God through Jesus Christ's sacrifice on the cross. In my own simple way, at the age of five, I started a relationship with God that has guided and transformed my life.

There is no other gift you can give your children as powerful and life-changing as the kind of introduction to faith in God that my parents gave me. I hope that someday your children will be able to say this with me: Thanks, Mom and Dad!

## Beliefs to Consider

- You need to choose beliefs that work for you— beliefs that motivate and enable the behaviors and results you want in your life.
- No one can dictate to you the beliefs by which to run your life.
- The beliefs you choose affect your behaviors and your results, and those affect your child.
- Change is about making a decision and cutting off beliefs and behaviors that are no longer useful, appropriate, and fitting for your life and the results you want.
- You have been transmitting beliefs to your child for his or her entire life.
- With new beliefs in place (or at least in process)

you can begin to purposefully convey those beliefs.

- Talk to your children about your beliefs and the beliefs they're developing.
- First, affirm and show love.
- Second, draw the line about right and wrong.
- Third, point to the larger, more important, belief.
- Fourth, talk about the beliefs—all the time.

# CHAPTER 14

# It's Time to Draw the Line!

Over and over during the past few months, I have heard people say, "It's time to draw a line in the sand."

Every time I hear that, I cringe. I know the phrase probably started with the idea of fighters making a challenge. But sand is the very last place you want to draw lasting lines.

Words have meaning, and that phrase sends a message to our unconscious mind about the nature of the boundary we are setting. Lines in sand are fleeting—they go away at the first wash of high waters or the first hint of a headwind.

It's time to stop drawing lines in the sand and time to start drawing some with indelible ink—ink like that of the Declaration of Independence and the Constitution.

It's time to stop drawing lines in the sand and time to start drawing them carved in stone—stone like that of the Ten Commandments and the words engraved in the Lincoln and Jefferson Memorials.

It's time to stop drawing lines in the sand and time to start drawing them in our hearts—so that we know our boundaries and can say, "Beyond this point, you shall not pass!"

Because if we don't decide, draw, and defend our own boundaries, someone else will do it for us.

# Postscript

Just as this book was going to press, I read of a new assault on children. Pedophiles from around the world have used Wikipedia, the online encyclopedia, to plant articles that portray adult-on-child sexual relations in a positive light. Their goal: to lure children into the pedophiles' world. An exclusive investigation by Fox News reported that they chose Wikipedia because public schools do not filter access to that site and most schools encourage students to do research there.

This article drove home to me just how pervasive the attacks on children are today. (If you wish to read the article, the link to the news report is in the Notes section.)

The focus of this book is on positive beliefs and tools—arming parents and children with morals, values, and character to make them strong and effective. But three things caused me to realize that you may need some defensive tools as well.

First, my research and articles like the one cited above have convinced me that attacks on our children are more viscous, calculated, and intense than I realized.

Second, I realized that even parents' best supervision and control may not keep their children out of harm's way. Many parents send their children to private or religious schools to protect them. Some parents go even further by choosing to home school their children. Some limit TV and computer time for their kids, filter the Internet, and choose which, if any, video games their children can play.

In spite of parents' valiant efforts to protect their children, sooner or later, those children are going to be exposed to the corrosive effects of the culture. Parents are justified in their efforts to hold off that day as long as possible, but it will come. Parents and children need to be armed for that day.

Third, through the years there have been voices in the nation that have spoken out—people who pushed back against darkness—against the beliefs and values that would destroy young people and tear apart the fabric of our nation. But, for whatever reason, that push back is fading.

Throughout this book, I've shown how the media, government, and schools often seem to have changed sides. The public outcry that would have pushed back against the changing of the lines seems muted.

To provide you help in building not only a strong offense but a strong defense, I've taken two steps.

First, I set up a website where we can meet at http://www.ICanDrawtheLine.com. Visit this site and find additional information for parents who want to arm themselves and their children to deal with these attacks. This website features articles, videos, and resources for parents and others who are concerned about our children and our nation. Feel free to leave your comments and suggestions.

Second, I set up a section on this site to provide defensive tools that parents can use and teach to their children. You can find this section of the website by looking for the "Tools" tab or by going directly to http://www.ICanDrawtheLine.com/Tools.

Talk to people you know—at school, at church, or at work—and ask them to stand with you *against* Belief Bankruptcy™ and *for* morality, values, and character that will nurture, support, and empower our children and our nation.

It's Time to Draw the Line!

# Remember; There's More!

**This book is only part of what I've put together for you.** My hope is that you will be increasingly successful with your children, so I have some additional resources waiting for you. These are free to purchasers of *It's Time to Draw the Line!*

**Demo Video**  First, you can watch a demonstration video that will show how to use many of the concepts presented here. Long after you finish reading this book, the video can remind you of what you can say and do to teach your children about beliefs, morality, values, and character. Access the video at:

**http://www.ICanDrawTheLine.com/demo**

**Webinars**  Second, you can access webinars in which I present additional resources for parents. In these webinars, you'll get more ideas, cutting edge strategies, to help you build powerful beliefs to pass on to your children. To register for these free webinars, go to:

**http://www.ICanDrawTheLine.com/webinars**

I hope that you will use and enjoy these additional resources. I wish only the best for you and your family!

RLHula

# Notes

**Page**

viii    Gallup poll:  May 17, 2010, http://www.
        gallup.com/poll/128042/Americans-Outlook-
        Morality-Remains-Bleak.aspx

3       KOMO online:  March 23, 2010, http://www.
        komonews.com/news/local/88971742.html

4       NYT Maureen Dowd column:  June 9, 2010,
        http://www.nytimes.com/2010/06/09/
        opinion/09dowd.html

23      Pew Research Poll:  April 18, 2010,
        http://people-press.org/report/606/
        trust-in-government

87      "Balancing Inquiry and Advocacy," Rick
        Ross and Charlotte Roberts, *Fifth Discipline
        Fieldbook,* Senge, et al, pg. 253, Senge,
        Roberts, Ross, Smith, Kleiner, Nicholas
        Brealey Publishing Ltd., London, 1994.

**Page**

127    *The Survivor's Club,* Ben Sherwood, pg. 139,
       Ben Sherwood, Grand Central Publishing,
       Hachette Book Group, New York, 2007.

133    FoxNews Wikipedia article:  June 25, 2010,
       http://www.foxnews.com/scitech/2010/06/25/
       exclusive-pedophiles-find-home-on-wikipedia/

# Acknowledgements

Thanks to the many parents I have learned from as I worked on this book. Your willingness to share is a gift to the future of our children and our nation.

Thanks to some wonderful mentors: Lowell Lytle, Robert Dilts, Robert Allen, Richard Paul Evans, and Joel Bauer. Each of you, in your own way, have helped me see the world and my abilities in a new way and have taught me how to communicate more effectively.

Thanks to Annette Jones, Heather Moore, Karen Christoffersen, and Bill Harrison for your input.

Thanks to my parents, John and Lorraine, who instilled in me a sense of curiosity and wonder about what makes the world work. Your beliefs sent me in the right direction and have served me well as a basis for building my own portfolio.

Special thanks to my wife, Nancy. This book would not have been possible without your work as an editor, graphic designer, and production expert. Your encouragement, support, and red pen marks have made every page better. Love always!

Rich
Hudson

Author

Speaker

Executive Coach

*The beliefs we hold have everything to do with the development of morality, values, and character.*

**Richard L. Hudson**

# About the Author

R ich Hudson is the BeliefBanker™, the country's top expert on The Most Important Investment You'll Ever Make™. He is an author, speaker, and executive coach who specializes in how to develop powerful beliefs to bring you the most important things in life.

Rich began studying hypnosis nearly 40 years ago and was introduced to the powerful role that beliefs play in personal achievement. His curiosity launched a life-long interest in beliefs, behavior, and how to get great results in life.

In 1972, Rich received a B.A. from Indiana University with a double major in Broadcast Communications and Music. His career in communications included work as a writer and producer, performer, composer and songwriter, recording engineer, and television audio director. He is an award-winning songwriter and was on the production team for two Emmy-award winning television programs.

In 1986, Rich began studying Neuro-Linguistic Programming (NLP) with the leaders in the field. Using this technology, Rich learned how to study internal strategies to identify the beliefs and behaviors that make an individual successful.

In 1990, Rich conducted a groundbreaking study of public speakers and identified the beliefs and behaviors that lead to confidence rather than fear. His two-day course, *Speak Your Mind—Without Losing It*™, teaches participants to become confident public speakers.

For six years Rich worked as an outside consultant for Hewitt Associates, training their consultants around the United States. In 1997, he joined Amadeus International, a global consultancy based in the United Kingdom. Rich has coached CEOs and Managing Directors on 4 continents and 14 countries for multinational corporations.

Rich now writes and speaks about Belief Investing™ and Belief Leadership™ as well as coaching and consulting with individuals and businesses.

To contact Rich about speaking to your group or organization, go to:

**http://www.RichardLHudson.com**

# Get in touch. Stay involved.

**t** Follow Rich on Twitter:
**http://twitter.com/RichardLHudson**

**f** Follow Rich on
Facebook:

Add . . .
**Richard L. Hudson**
. . . as your Facebook friend.

Connect . . .
**It's Time to Draw the Line**
. . . Facebook fan page.

Join BeliefBank™
Connection

**http://www.BeliefBank.com/**
**Connection**
Receive exclusive book updates,
online gifts, event information
and other great benefits all
FREE.